THE CATHOLIC BIBLE STUDY HANDBOOK

THE CATHOLIC BIBLE STUDY HANDBOOK

Jerome Kodell, O.S.B.

Second Revised Edition

PUBLISHED BY ST. ANTHONY MESSENGER PRESS
CINCINNATI, OHIO

Published by St. Anthony Messenger Press
28 W. Liberty St.
Cincinnati, OH 45202
www.servantbooks.com

Cover design by Paul Higdon - Minneapolis, MN

04 10 9 8 7 6 5 4

Printed in the United States of America
ISBN 0-56955-267-3

Library of Congress Cataloging-in-Publication Data

Kodell, Jerome.
    The Catholic Bible study handbook / Jerome Kodell.—2nd rev. ed.
        p. cm.
    Includes bibliographical references and index.
    ISBN 0-89283-185-5
    1. Bible—Study and teaching—Handbooks, manuals, etc. 2. Bible—Study and
teaching—Catholic Church—Handbooks, manuals, etc. I. Title.

    BS417 .K63 2001
    220.6'1—dc21

                                                          2001017364

Contents

"Do you really understand what you are reading?" Philip asked. The Ethiopian looked up from the book of Isaiah and answered, "How can I, unless someone guides me?"

This exchange took place on the road from Gaza to Jerusalem almost 2,000 years ago (Acts 8:26-39). But it could equally well occur in countless places today, as men and women try to understand the Bible. Were someone like Philip to ask them, "Do you really understand what you are reading?" they would probably give the same answer as the Ethiopian: "How can I, unless someone guides me?" They might add, "I do pretty well with the Gospels and some of Paul's letters, but Hebrews is Greek to me and the Book of Revelation is a complete puzzle. And as for the Old Testament, well ..."

No one should be ashamed of being sometimes perplexed by the Bible. If it were a book that was everywhere easy to understand, the Ethiopian would not have needed help, and God would not have had to send Philip to help him. Even though the Bible is the word of God and God wishes to speak his word to everyone, this does not mean that everyone can simply sit down and completely understand his word at first reading.

It is not that God wants to make his word complicated or hard to understand. Our difficulties stem from the fact that God has chosen to speak to us in human words, and speak to us at length.

To take the second fact first: God has blessed us with an abundance of revelation. The Bible is really not a book but a library. Like any library, it takes us some time to find our way around in it. None of the books in this divine library stands completely on its own, but each takes on its full meaning in the context of everything else that God has said. Unless we have some overview of the entire contents of this library, the point of many of the individual books will remain elusive and some of them will be downright puzzling.

An even more basic difficulty we will encounter in trying to understand the Bible is that God has chosen to speak to us through human words—inspired human words, to be sure, but fully human words nonetheless. God chose to speak through authors who wrote as men of their own time and world, even though they were writing eternal truths. We live in a different time and world and have to journey back to theirs to understand what they said.

What do I mean by this? Well, imagine that Jeremiah and Paul were to drop by for breakfast and join you in reading the morning newspaper. How much of what they read would they understand? What questions would they ask you as you studied the headlines and main stories, skimmed the sports pages, and tore out grocery coupons? Obviously the world has changed a great deal since they lived, and many things that you take for granted as common knowledge would be unknown to them.

Something of the reverse is also true as we read words written by Jeremiah and Paul and all the other inspired human authors and editors of Scripture. The worlds of the Old and New Testament were different from our world, and many things these authors took for granted are matters that have to be explained to us: matters of geography and history, culture and custom, politics and religious practice. We should no more expect to comprehend what Jeremiah and Paul wrote without some knowledge of these matters than we should expect Jeremiah and Paul to be able to understand this morning's newspaper without some knowledge of our modern world.

It would be of immeasurable help to us if we had Jeremiah and Paul sitting by our side as we read their writings. We could ask them to explain the background of what they said and the meaning of what they wrote. Or lacking their presence, we would be very grateful if Philip were to drop by as we read our Bibles and explain what we were reading, as he explained a prophecy from Isaiah to the Ethiopian.

I do not want to give the impression, however, that without Jeremiah, Paul, or Philip at our side it is pointless to try to understand the Bible. That is definitely not true. The more we read the Bible, the more we will understand it. The historical books of the Old Testament will give us the background that will help us understand the prophets of the Old Testament, and our understanding of the prophets will in turn bring a new depth of meaning to our reading of the New Testament. Even if we were left on the proverbial desert island with nothing but the text of the Bible, there would be enough for us to learn to keep us occupied for many, many years.

Fortunately, we are not stranded on desert islands or left to cope with the complexities of Scripture on our own. Many helpful guides to the Bible are available today that can make Scripture more understandable to us, and prevent us from wandering down many a blind alley. *The Catholic Bible Study Handbook* by Abbot Jerome Kodell, O.S.B., is one of them. He surveys the library that is the Bible in order to provide us with the overview we need to find our way around in it. He describes the times in which the books of the Bible were written and edited, and thus gives us background for understanding them. He takes up such practical questions as why Catholic and Protestant Bibles contain a different number of books, and he provides a particularly clear evaluation of modern translations of Scripture.

Quite importantly, he gives pointers for studying the Bible as individuals and in groups, and for using the Bible as a springboard for prayer.

Abbot Kodell does not particularly recommend that you sit down and read this handbook from cover to cover—but if you have the time, it's not a bad idea. The central chapters of this handbook provide a sweeping survey of both biblical times and the books of the Bible. Such a survey can be like gazing at a meandering valley from a mountaintop before attempting to walk its length: you will still need to make your way through some thickets and across several streams, but at least you will know the broad outlines of your journey.

Others may prefer to make more selective use of this handbook, reading what it has to say about a particular book of Scripture before setting out to read the book itself, and consulting such chapters as those on prayer and group study when they are of particular interest. However you use this handbook, it should help you grow in your understanding of Scripture so that you can hear its message as the word of God to you.

George Martin

Preface to the Second Revised Edition

A major fruit of Vatican Council II has been the return to the Bible for personal spiritual guidance and nourishment at all levels in the Roman Catholic Church. This has been most marked in the case of the millions of lay Catholics who have made regular personal and group Bible reading and study, in the context of prayer, a staple of their spiritual journey.

The present handbook was published sixteen years ago as a source of basic biblical information for home and parish study. I received a lot of help at the time in determining what to include from developers and participants in the Little Rock Scripture Study program, with which I had been involved since its inception in 1974. I am very happy that the book has been a helpful resource over the years and that its continuing usefulness is signaled by Servant Publications' decision to publish this revised edition.

Much has happened in the world of Catholic biblical study in the years since the first edition of this book. Many new resources have appeared to assist Catholic home and parish Bible study, including other handbooks and new study programs. These will be referenced in the final section as part of the updating of this edition. There has been a deepening awareness of the priority of approaching the Bible as a source of prayer and union with God rather than mainly as a focus of doctrinal debate, especially in the rediscovery of the rich approaches of the *lectio divina*—"inspired reading"—tradition.

The Catholic student of the Bible has been immeasurably strengthened in these years by the appearance in 1993 of a document produced by the Pontifical Biblical Commission entitled *The Interpretation of the Bible in the Church*. The document presents an overview of approaches to the Bible, describing the principal methods used at the current time, and situates them within the tradition of Catholic interpretation. The text repays close study as a kind of minicourse in solid Bible interpretation.

What about the material presented in the main chapters of the book? What changes and adaptations have been required for this new edition? Since the original purpose of the book was to gather the generally uncontested conclusions of Catholic biblical research, it did not venture into speculative questions. I have found it necessary to modify very little or nothing in the chapters of sections one and two, "What Is the Bible?" and "Background to the Bible."

However, I might mention two areas where there has been some ferment, but not enough to warrant a change in the positions adopted in the text, and where there are no evident doctrinal implications in a choice one way or another. In chapter 3, I present the theory of the composition of the Pentateuch in terms of the four traditions identified as the Yahwist (J), Elohist (E), Deuteronomist (D), and Priestly (P). There has been critique of this theory, but it is recognized as reflecting the complex process of production of the Pentateuch, and no other theory has won nearly the same scholarly acceptance, Catholic or otherwise.

In chapter 8, I describe the relationships of the three synoptic Gospels in terms of the priority of Mark, which has long been the accepted principle by the vast majority of modern commentators. Evidence for the priority of Matthew, or at least evidence of textual difficulties with Marcan priority, continues to be adduced by a strong minority of scholars, so that the consensus does not seem as unshaken as before.

An issue which goes beyond the focus of this book but which has attracted much media attention in the last decade is research about the historical Jesus. On its beneficial side, this research gets us closer to the reality of Jesus in his historical, cultural, and social context. Such research becomes dangerous when the available sources are pushed for information beyond their capabilities or when information about Jesus and his teaching from noncanonical sources (such as those mentioned in chapter 9) is given equal weight in argument with the canonical Gospels.

My prayer is that in its updated version, this handbook will serve Bible readers who are just beginning a deeper study of the holy word as well as veterans who may dip into it to check on details from time to time.

Acknowledgments

Chapter 3 is taken with modifications from the Catholic study edition of the *Good News Bible,* 1979, with permission of William H. Sadlier, Inc., publisher. Old Testament: copyright American Bible Society, 1976. New Testament: copyright American Bible Society, 1966, 1971, 1976.

Material in chapter 11 from *God's Word Today* of April 1982. Copyright *God's Word Today,* 1982. Material in chapter 11 also from *New Covenant* of November 1983. Copyright The National Service Committee of the Catholic Charismatic Renewal of the United States, Inc., 1983.

Part I

What Is the Bible?

ONE

Why Read the Bible?

Why read the Bible? If you're not a regular Bible reader it's probably because you haven't found a compelling reason to be one. A Catholic might ask: "Why should I read the Bible, when the Church tells me all I need to believe about God and salvation?" But the very fact that you have picked up this book is a sign that you are interested in the Bible and are looking for a reason for reading and studying it.

Or it might be that you are already a Bible reader, looking for ways to deepen your appreciation and knowledge of Scripture. Not all the reasons people have for reading the Bible are of equal value. One could read it as an ancient source of religious knowledge or because of its insights into the mystery of God and the meaning of existence. Some people read the Bible because of the helpful guidance and advice it provides for daily living (though only parts of the Bible are suitable for that). Other reasons come from church authority, or family tradition, or the personal appeal of a powerful teacher or evangelist. But most of us are looking for a reason from "inside" the Bible, from its very nature, a reason that applies to all of the biblical writings all of the time. If the Bible is unique, there must be a unique reason for reading it. The answer lies in the areas of revelation and inspiration.

Revelation

Revelation means the uncovering or disclosure of something that was hidden. When a solution to problems or an explanation of mysterious circumstances pops suddenly into our minds, we often call it a revelation. We don't know where it came from; certainly it bypassed our normal reasoning channels. Did it come from God? Sometimes we are sure it did, at other times not so sure. The human mind has surprising natural capabilities. When we apply the term *revelation* to the Bible, we are speaking in a stricter sense of divine revelation, the communication of truth from God. Ultimately, divine revelation is truth we wouldn't get any other way.

Our Christian faith is based on revelation. We believe that God has communicated to us the truth about himself and about the purpose of our existence. This comes to us in and through Jesus Christ, who is divine revelation in human form. Everything that God wants his people to know about himself and his purposes is contained in the life and teaching of Jesus. Knowledge of this revelation is not restricted to the Bible, of course. St. Peter never read one of the Gospels in our Bible, but he received God's revelation in the person of Jesus, through his life in the Christian community, through his prayer, through the Holy Spirit. The same is true today. God is not limited in his revelation. He speaks to anyone anywhere according to his own will. But he has given the Bible as a privileged source of his revelation.

We would already be misled at this point if revelation were taken to mean primarily certain facts or truths about God and religion. Revelation is primarily God's personal communication of *himself* to his children. You might know everything about

God, but not know God; you would not have received his revelation. God's plan is part of revelation, but it is the second part. The first part is God himself. The Catholic bishops at Vatican Council II put it this way in their *Constitution on Divine Revelation* (*1965*): "In his goodness and wisdom God chose to reveal himself and to make known to us the hidden purpose of his will by which through Christ, the Word made flesh, people have access to the Father in the Holy Spirit and come to share in the divine nature. Through this revelation, therefore, the invisible God out of the abundance of his love speaks to his people as friends and lives among them, so that he may invite and take them into fellowship with himself" [section 2].

Because the Bible contains divine revelation, it is a place to meet God and to learn his plan for the world and for ourselves. Here we address the real reason for Bible reading: as revelation in its most authentic written form, the Bible is a privileged place for an encounter with God. God may be met in a sunset, a moving experience, another person; but the Bible is a sure place, like one of the sacraments of the Church. God is always present in his revealed word, eager to meet his children. A later passage in the *Constitution on Divine Revelation* stresses this point: "Inspired by God and committed once and for all to writing, the Scriptures impart the word of God himself without change, and make the voice of the Holy Spirit resound in the words of the prophets and apostles. Therefore, like the Christian religion itself, all the preaching of the Church must be nourished and ruled by sacred Scripture. For in the sacred books, the Father who is in heaven meets his children with great love and speaks with them" [section 21].

Inspiration

What does it mean to be "inspired by God"? Inspiration has var
ious nonreligious meanings. There are inspired speakers who
move us to action by their eloquence and personal conviction.
Literary inspiration is the gift of our great poets and novelists. A
critic can tell by the quality of the speaking performance or the
literary product of a writer whether this kind of inspiration was
present.

Divine inspiration is both similar and different. It is similar in
that where divine inspiration is present there is a power at work.
But a divinely inspired action or speech or writing may not be
moving or even particularly noticeable. A divinely inspired writing may even be dull and (poetically) uninspiring. Divine inspiration means that God involves himself in a special way in a
human event, guaranteeing his presence and the truth of what
is communicated. When God inspires, he works within the
human history he has created and with the creatures he has
formed, but he protects these fragile creations from error in
establishing his truth.

The Bible is a divinely inspired writing. Biblical inspiration
means that the Scriptures make God's presence available to the
readers and that the Bible will teach only truth about the ultimate realities of life and salvation. Biblical inspiration guarantees
that the Bible contains God's authentic revelation about himself
and his plan for the world. It assures readers that they are in the
presence of God and his truth when opening the Bible in faith.

There are different theories about how biblical inspiration
worked in the production of the Bible. Was St. Paul inspired, for
instance, in everything he wrote; and if so, what if we were to
find one of his lost letters? In the case of certain books (like

Genesis) which went through several editions over centuries before they reached their present form, were each of the contributing writers inspired or only the final editor? Or was it the communities in which these writers lived that were inspired? All such questions are provocative but do not affect the promise which biblical inspiration brings to the Bible reader: however it came about, the book we have before us was produced under God's inspiration, and has all the qualities which divine inspiration provides.

Transforming Power

Today's Christians seem as convinced as believers of any age of the importance of the Bible as a criterion of doctrinal truth. Some carry this to the extreme of making it the only criterion. At any rate, biblical inspiration's effect of ensuring the Bible's faithfulness to the divine revelation is widely recognized and accepted among all Christians. But the other effects of inspiration are often minimized at great loss to believers. This is especially true of the healing and saving power of the word of God which the Bible contains because of God's presence.

A striking ceremony opened the first session of the Council of Ephesus in the year A.D. 431. The presiding bishop carried the book of the Scriptures to the head of the assembly and enthroned it between candles. The book was then incensed and treated with all the deference due a king. One of the fathers of that council, Cyril of Alexandria, explained the meaning of this ceremony in a letter to Emperor Theodosius: "The holy synod assembled together in the church and gave Christ, as it were, membership in the presidency of the council. For the venerable

Gospel was placed on a holy throne." The practice witnessed to the Christian belief that Jesus Christ is present in the divinely inspired Bible. This enthronement of the Bible has continued down to our own day. At each general session of Vatican Council II, one of the bishops carried the Holy Book in procession to its place of enthronement. The *Constitution on Divine Revelation* quoted earlier recalled the ancient Christian tradition of reverence for the written word of God: "The Church has always venerated the divine Scriptures just as she venerates the body of the Lord, since from the table of both the word of God and of the body of Christ she unceasingly receives and offers to the faithful the Bread of Life, especially in the sacred liturgy" [section 21].

Though the doctrinal importance of the Bible has been maintained, this effect of biblical inspiration—the presence and power of the word—has been obscured in recent times. A main reason for this is a change in our understanding of the concept *word. Word* for the ancients was primarily something spoken, not written, containing an individual's force of personality and authority. This spoken word was stronger than any written word. It was used to seal contracts; if a person broke his word, he somehow broke himself. In our time, a written word is considered more significant than a spoken one. In our eyes, written evidence is more convincing than a personal word. This makes it difficult for us to understand what the Bible means by the word of God and why this word does more than proclaim the truth.

The concept of *word* underlying the biblical writings comes from the ancient Hebrews. In their way of thinking, a word is more than the expression of an idea; it may be a happening. They had a single term, *dabar*, to mean word, thing, and event.

Isaac's servant, for example, told his master "all the words he had done" (Gn 24:66), meaning his journeying and the winning of Rebekah. Spoken words contained the energy and personality of the speaker. Special words, like blessings and curses, were so strong that they were independent from the speaker. Once Isaac had released the blessing for his firstborn son, he could not bring it back, even though he had been deceived into awarding it to the wrong son (Gn 27:35).

The word of the Lord is even more powerful and independent. When it comes from on high, something happens. It is like the rain which waters the earth, making it fertile and fruitful:

> So shall my word be
> > that goes forth from my mouth;
> It shall not return to me void,
> > but shall do my will,
> > achieving the end for which I sent it.
>
> ISAIAH 55:10-11

The prophets were bearers of God's word. It changed their lives, not by challenging only their minds, but by stunning them with God's saving power. Jeremiah spoke of God's word as a "fire burning in my heart, imprisoned in my bones" (Jer 20:9). Ezekiel ate a scroll to symbolize the entry of God's word into his life (Ez 3:1-4); Isaiah had his lips seared by a coal from the altar (Is 6:5-7).

Jesus is described as the Word of God made flesh (Jn 1:14); he and his message reach beyond the mind to the very heart of men and women: "Indeed, the word of God is living and effective, sharper than any two-edged sword, penetrating even between soul and spirit, joints and marrow, and able to discern reflections and thoughts of the heart" (Heb 4:12). Jesus describes his spoken word as a seed (Mk 4:1-20). Like a seed, the word has the power of life in itself. It does not grow magically any more than does a grain of wheat, but when the conditions are right, new life comes forth and flourishes.

God's word, in whatever form it comes, always has divine healing and saving power. The seven sacraments of the Church are the most vivid and direct proclamations of God's healing word in Christ. The risen Lord Jesus acts in them to extend his healing touch to the minds, hearts, and bodies of the disciples. Where the conditions are right, that is, where a heart is open in faith, the seed of God's word takes root and has a sure effect. The same kind of divine power is available through God's written word in the Bible; the effect of individual readings is not as clearly defined, but the healing power of God is present. It is "the word of God, which is now at work in you who believe" (1 Thes 2:13).

The day-to-day effect of Bible reading is usually subtle but real. The divine power does not work only through striking ideas or feelings, so the Bible reader cannot measure the effect of the Scriptures as the spiritual life grows. But from time to time the transforming power of the word of God is recognized as one's life becomes more peaceful, joyful, whole.

A story from the early Church clarifies this point. In the fourth and fifth centuries the deserts of Egypt were populated by men and women who had gone into the wilderness to seek God in solitary prayer. Many of these Christian monastics became very holy and were sought out by other searchers for advice. A young man came to one of the monks and made his request: "Father, I want to seek God in this wilderness, too. How can I become holy and happy?" "My son," said the Desert

Father, "go over into one of those caves, taking with you this book of Scriptures. Read it day and night and you will find what you are seeking." After three days, the young man returned, complaining that the reading was boring, that his mind wandered, and that he remembered little of what he read. "Do not despair, my son. You are doing fine. But do this also. Fill a basket with sand and set it just outside your cave. Every morning and evening pour a bucket of water over the sand. Come back in a week and we will talk." The young monk followed the older man's strange instructions. At the end of the week he still complained about his lack of progress in holy reading. "But about the sand, every time I pour water over it, some leaks out the sides of the basket." This same simple process continued, with the young monk coming each week to talk with his spiritual father. Finally he reported: "Father, the sand is all gone. For the past two days I have been pouring water into a clean basket. But with the reading, I find myself just as lazy and bored and forgetful as ever." The old man rose. "My son, you are the basket. The sand is your sinfulness, pride, unhappiness. The water is the word of God. The basket doesn't remember the water that gradually cleansed it. No more do you remember every word of holy Scripture that you read. But if you continue to pour the water of God's word over your sinfulness every day, some day you too will be clean."

This is why the Bible is worth reading. Its healing and transforming power is the revelation we all seek, whether we recognize the fact or not. Regular Bible reading will strengthen our knowledge of revealed truth. But most of all, it will deepen our relationship with the Father, Son, and Holy Spirit and cleanse us for ever closer union with God. One final reference to Vatican II's *Constitution on Divine Revelation* will complete an earlier quotation and summarize the message of this chapter: "In the sacred books, the Father who is in heaven meets his children with great love and speaks with them; and the force and power in the word of God is so great that it remains the support and energy of the Church, the strength of faith for her children, the food of the soul, the pure and perennial source of spiritual life" [section 21].

TWO

Hearing God's Word
in the Bible

Studying the Bible isn't as simple as it sounds. If it were, there wouldn't be so many different ideas about its meaning. Everywhere there are signs of division and conflict over the Bible. One preacher says this, another that; neighbors united in everything else belong to different churches because of disagreements over biblical interpretation. It is one thing to be convinced that Bible reading is a good spiritual practice; it is another to know a sound and sure way to make Bible reading work for me. The Bible proclaims the word of God, granted; but surely all these divisions and bickerings do not come from God. Not everyone who reads the Bible hears the word of God in it. How can I be sure that what I find in the inspired Scriptures is the word of God and not some mere human word, perhaps the echo of my own thoughts?

Besides these common anxieties, a Catholic might have further hesitations about Bible reading. Hasn't our Church warned time and again about "private interpretation" and about the need for guidance in Scripture reading and study? Most Catholics of middle age and more remember very little use of the Bible in their religious training. The catechism, we were told, is enough—and, in fact, for our education in religious doctrine, it was. Because of this, the exaggerated stories about Bible reading being forbidden to Catholics seem to have the ring of truth.

But they are not true. The Catholic Church has always revered the Bible as the inspired word of God. The Catholic fathers and doctors and Church councils through the centuries have spoken eloquently of the crucial role of the Scriptures in the life of the Church. The writings of the great saints bear witness to the importance of the Bible in their spiritual journeys. It is true that after the Protestant Reformation in the sixteenth century, when the Body of Christ experienced division and splintering through differences in biblical interpretation, the Catholic Church became very protective. Private interpretation was a main cause of Christian division, so it became the subject of strong admonitions and warning.

Private Interpretation

Private interpretation of biblical doctrine is not the same as personal reading of the Bible for spiritual growth. Though the Church warns against private doctrinal interpretation—and will continue to do so—personal use of Scripture is encouraged. The texts for the Mass and sacraments and private devotions are composed in large part of biblical readings and of prayers inspired by biblical themes and images. The doctrinal truth of divine revelation is not for me as an individual believer to determine; but God's personal message to me is mine to hear and understand. Though there are aids in hearing God's word, no one else can listen to God for me. Today, the Church continues to protect the doctrinal interpretation of Scripture as a matter beyond the decision of individual readers, but at the same time, in the strongest language encourages the personal, private reading and study of the sacred texts. If the inspired word is read in a spirit of faith and prayer, the Holy Spirit will protect from error and lead the reader to God's true message for his or her life.

Later in this book more will be said about ways of reading and studying the Bible, in groups and individually. But before that can happen, the issue of doctrinal interpretation needs to be dealt with more thoroughly. When interpretation is seen in its proper light, there will be a better context for understanding how an individual may use the Bible for great personal profit without fear of falling into mistakes and divisions.

The Question of Authority

The critical word here is *authority*. Who has the authority to decide the proper doctrinal interpretation of Scripture passages? Many Christians maintain that this authority belongs to the individual believer. Catholics maintain that this authority was given by Jesus to his followers as a group under their proper leaders. In other words, the authority to decide what is the saving truth and what is the norm of Christian living revealed by the Bible is vested in the Church with its appointed leaders.

An example may help to focus the point at issue. In chapter 13 of John's Gospel, Jesus washes the feet of his disciples at the Last Supper. In commenting on this action, the Master says to them: "If I, therefore, the master and teacher, have washed your feet, you ought to wash one another's feet. I have given you a model to follow, so that as I have done for you, you should also do" (Jn 13:14-15). There is scarcely any other passage in the Gospels, unless it is the institution of the Eucharist, where such precise instructions are given by Jesus to his followers: "As I have done for you, you should also do." But how many Christians wash one another's feet?

Most Gospel readers probably interpret "washing one another's feet" as a symbol of service to others, an encouragement to love in action or humility in doing good to others. "I don't need to wash feet literally to fulfill this command; I do it by serving others." Fine—but who tells you that you may interpret the text this way? There is nothing in the reading itself to indicate that Jesus did not mean a physical washing of physical feet. Your authority for reading the text that way is not coming from the Bible but from outside it.

The Catholic admits this. The Bible does not interpret itself but needs an authentic interpreter. This, for the Catholic, is the community of believers, the Church, guided by the Holy Spirit through its leaders. It is not up to individual whim. The believer who accepts no Church authority in interpretation, but professes to follow the Bible literally as it stands, cannot take a passage like John 13 symbolically and be consistent, because such an interpretation implies a nonbiblical criterion. Yet the believer who interprets the passage in a literalistic way will end up bowing to an authority which has not been identified: a particular preacher or author, a group of believers, a personal preference. When the authority I am following has not been identified, I suffer from the illusion that I am acting on my own, independent of any outside norm. In practice, I am usually flitting from one unidentified authority to another, a bee in search of the sweetest nectar. In the case of the Bible, this leads to inconsistency in interpretation, and eventually to division.

The Brothers and Sisters of Jesus

Another example, Mark 6:3, speaks of the "brothers" and "sisters" of Jesus. Catholics interpret this to mean his cousins, which is consistent with the doctrine of Mary's perpetual virginity. Some other Christians interpret this to mean his siblings, blood brothers and sisters. They say that Mary was a virgin up to the birth of Jesus, but later had other children by the natural fatherhood of Joseph. Which interpretation is correct?

To the reader of English the question might seem very easy: why take the terms *brother* and *sister* to mean anything different from what they ordinarily mean for us? But the Bible cannot interpret itself here, because the underlying Aramaic terms for brother and sister are ambiguous: they may mean cousin as well as brother or sister. The decision whether the terms here mean cousins or siblings has important doctrinal implications. Who has the authority to make this decision? Whichever decision is made cannot come from the Bible itself, which is ambiguous on the point.

The Catholic looks to the authority of the Church, which has a constant tradition about Mary's perpetual virginity handed down from the earliest times. This is a question of historical fact, and when the Bible is ambiguous about such things, the only valid recourse is historical tradition. This again points to the importance of the Church's authority in biblical interpretation and to the danger of following, without realizing it, an unidentified authority. An unidentified norm of interpretation may well be Christian, but it may just as well be hostile or indifferent to Christianity, such as prejudice, materialism, or American common sense.

Literalism

We touch here on another widespread danger in biblical interpretation: the judgment of a particular text at face value as it appears at this time, without reference to other teachings on the same point, to the context, or to the particular language usages that could affect the meaning. This is often referred to by its practitioners as "literal" or "fundamental" interpretation. The Bible is taken at its literal word. But it is more properly termed "literalist" because attention is to the letter on the surface rather than to the meaning underneath. A literalist, for example, would respond to a report of "raining pitchforks" with iron umbrellas. The authority behind this kind of interpretation is hidden because the interpreter will not admit it: the authority is one's own imagination, ingenuity, and system of preferences.

Another example will help to clarify the problem of literalist interpretation. Once when I was attending an interdenominational revival, the text for a particular sermon was the saying of Jesus in John 10:10: "I came so that they might have life and have it more abundantly." The preacher proceeded to tell us that this meant that all true followers of Jesus could count on material prosperity and security, good mental and physical health, and happy family and social relationships. He gave the impression that anyone in the audience suffering from some sickness or tragedy was lacking in faith and love of God. Where did he get his interpretation? There is nothing in the context of the Gospel of John or in other teachings of Jesus to support this interpretation. In fact, it evades the whole issue of suffering and the cross, which is central to the life and message of Jesus. The preacher could point to the text and say: "It's right here in the text; what else could 'abundant life' mean?" But he was projecting his own thoughts and priorities into the Bible, and what he drew from the text was not the inspired word of God but a reflection of his own mind.

The Church and the Bible

Christians need authoritative guidance in searching the Scriptures for doctrinal truth. People are not easily convinced of this. "I can read the Bible for myself" is a constant refrain. But the undeniable fact is that the Bible was given not simply to individual believers but to the community of believers, the Church, as a source of truth and life. The Church existed before the Bible; the word of God was living and active in the Christian community in many ways before it became available in written form. Protestants sometimes express the feeling that Catholics are limited in their freedom because they belong to a church which proclaims and defines the doctrines to be believed. But the Church, under the Spirit's guidance and inspiration, has been commissioned with the task of discerning for its people the path of life. Knowing the divinely appointed boundaries of belief gives more, rather than less, freedom to a Christian. It cuts out a million worries and questions. Flannery O'Connor, the late Catholic novelist, referred to dogma (a defined doctrine) as a "gateway to contemplation."

As important as the Bible is in the life of believers, it is not the only source of God's word. This has been said before but bears repetition. Our Father is a living God still speaking a living word. He continues to speak to his people in infinitely varied ways: in prayer, through nature and world events, in daily life and relationships. He is not speaking only to his own people but to the whole world. But his community of followers, his Church, is commissioned to be the interpreter of his word for the world.

The disciples of Jesus heard God's word before there was a New Testament. Saints Peter and Paul probably never read a Gospel; and they had access to few of the documents we presently revere as God's word in Christ. The New Testament was produced by the Church under the inspiration of the Holy Spirit. Therefore the Bible is the Church's book. The Church wrote it, and the Church interprets it through the ages under the guidance of the same Holy Spirit who helped her write it in the first place. The understanding of God's word is handed down in the Church from generation to generation. This is what is meant by tradition, a handing on of the deep awareness of God's truth revealed to the apostles and teachers. Tradition is not a sort of side channel of revelation, a collection of secret teachings and practices passed along through the years; it is the ongoing interpretation of the revelation given to the Church in the apostolic age.

This approach to the Bible explains how the Church can proclaim doctrines which are not mentioned explicitly in Scripture, such as the Marian doctrines of the Immaculate Conception and the Assumption, or the doctrine of purgatory. Church teaching is derived from God's word to the Church especially as articulated in the inspired writings. But the Church is not limited to the exact expression of the truth as it appears in the Bible. The Church does not depend on the Bible alone for what it believes; if it did, during the decades before the New Testament was completed Christians would have had nothing to believe. The Church will never teach anything contradictory to the Scriptures, but it may draw out implications that are not superficially evident. The Holy Spirit's continuing inspiration of the Church occasionally leads to a conclusion that is not explicitly stated in Scripture.

The Humanness of the Word

The Church does not exercise its interpretive commission in a freewheeling sort of way. Even under the Spirit, the Church must, like each Christian, take the strenuous steps necessary for authentic interpretation. A basic conviction in Catholic interpretation (which may sound self-evident but is not accepted by all Christians) is that the Bible is and remains, even though blessed by God's inspiration, a human word produced by human effort. God did not sidestep the humanness of the biblical authors when he guided them to produce the Scriptures. The best methods available to understand any human writing must be applied to the biblical text.

Each piece of writing must be treated with respect for what it is. A gospel is not a psalm, a parable is not a history, a religious statement is not a biological statement (which is the mistake Nicodemus made: Jn 3:4). The language of the author, the context of his times, and the pressures of the time in which he wrote may bear on the meaning of the text. The number 666 in Revelation 13:18 can be applied to anyone at any time if the interpreter is unaware that, at the time John wrote, Nero Caesar was the only possibility. Words and sentences in the Bible as in other human writings are not free-floating; they have a context. Without attention to the context, a Bible reader could believe "There is no God" (Ps 14:1).

In an often quoted paragraph in the *Constitution on the Liturgy,* the bishops of Vatican Council II called attention to the various ways Christ is present in the Christian assembly: in his people, in the minister, in the bread and wine, in the sacraments, in the word. The sentence describing his presence in the Scriptures reads: "He is present in his word, since it is he himself who speaks when the holy Scriptures are read in the Church" [section 7]. The words "in the Church" do not mean inside the church building. Reading the Scriptures in the Church is reading them in faith and in continuity with the belief and teaching of the Church through the centuries and now. Biblical words, like any others, may be taken out of context; without the control of faith and proper teaching authority, what we read in the Bible may not be the word of God at all. But when it is read "in the Church" in faith, Christ is present in his word with saving power and solid truth.

THREE

How the Bible Came About

Though the Bible may look like any other book on a desk or shelf, it is more like a library in itself than just another book. It is a collection of many different writings by several authors produced over hundreds of years. As in a library, the books of the Bible are not simply stacked one after another in the order in which they were produced, but they are arranged carefully according to their topic. For instance, Genesis is placed first because it deals with the creation of the world and man's early history, not because it was the first book to be written. Revelation is placed last because it deals with the "last things"—the end of the world, the final judgment, and the heavenly reign at the end of time.

The individual books in the Bible are significantly different from books produced today. Most modern books are written by a single author within a period of a few weeks, months, or possibly years. Few of the biblical books, especially those in the Old Testament, came to us straight from the pen of an individual writer. Many of them were edited and reedited over the course of several generations. A prophet like Isaiah was more likely to speak the word of God than to write it down; he left the task of writing to his disciples. They, in turn, might have produced only random notes of what Isaiah said. Later followers organized those notes and put them into a smoother written style.

This participation of many different people, sometimes over a period of many years and in more than one place, in the production of a certain writing is a major characteristic of the Bible. With few exceptions, the authors of the Old and New Testament books did not think of themselves as professional writers. They were members of a community which felt itself to be especially chosen as the bearer of God's promise. Their writing was an expression of the community in action: it was the result of the process of listening to God's word in history and in the religious experience of the nation, of reflecting on that word, of telling the story, and of handing on the message to later generations of the community. Thus, the writings and the stories they tell are understood to be the property of the entire community, not just the author. It is no matter that the identity of the authors may be blurred; and there is no anxiety about preserving an individual writer's words intact. The Bible comes from the midst of the community of faith in order to serve the community of faith.

The ancients did not share our contemporary understanding of authorship. For them, the writing was the important thing; who wrote it was secondary. We are surprised at the anonymity of so many books of the Bible; the ancients would not have been. What is even more amazing to us is the ancient practice of attributing books to famous people of the present or the past. This was done both to encourage the reading of the book and to protect the book itself. In a time when books were handwritten, it was relatively easy to change existing copies, or even to destroy them. But an important name on a manuscript—an emperor's, for instance—would lend it some security.

We know that biblical authors often wrote under the names of earlier heroes of the faith: Moses, David, Solomon, Peter,

Paul, John. Some of the writings attributed to these great figures came directly from them, but some did not. Usually, the anonymous writer tried to transmit the thought of the earlier leader or author, even imitating language and style, bringing ancient truth to bear on a new situation. There is no dishonesty involved here, nor is there any challenge to divine inspiration. The word of God comes through known and unknown writers. The books of the Bible are inspired, whether we know who wrote them or not.

The ancient concept of history was also much different from ours. The modern notion of scientific history, worked out in its main lines during the last few centuries, puts the emphasis on the accurate recording of facts and figures. For the ancients, eliciting the meaning of events was more important than accurately recording them. As long as the main story line was clear, names and facts might be added or omitted here and there.

A modern historical writer gathers the facts and draws from them his or her conclusions about the movement and meaning of events. The biblical historians began with the conclusion (based of course on historical events) that God is working in history to save his people. They then used the facts to illustrate this truth. This approach gave them freedom in recording names, dates, and places. A story about Abraham could be repeated of Isaac (Gn 20:1-18; 26:6-11); Goliath's death could be attributed to two different people (1 Sm 17:51; 2 Sm 21:19); the cleansing of the Temple could be situated either at the beginning or at the end of Jesus' public career (Jn 2:13-22; Mk 11:15-17). This different concept of historical writing has caused modern readers to raise problems where the biblical authors saw none.

Old Testament

Earliest Writings. From the time of Abraham, the Israelites were a nomadic people. The nomads of the ancient Near East had little room for carrying written scrolls. They carried their library in their heads. The ancient Hebrews, like all people who depend on oral traditions instead of written documents to preserve their history, developed amazingly retentive memories. Their storytellers put the saga of their ancestors into poetic rhythm. Their songs of worship were easy to remember because they repeated the same ideas and phrases. For the first 500 years of their existence the Israelites shared their history and passed along their traditions almost exclusively by word of mouth.

It was not until the nation became a settled kingdom under David and Solomon that a national written literature began to emerge, even though there are fragments of biblical writing that reach much further back in time. Some of the earliest parts of the Old Testament are snatches of the ancient Hebrew religious ballads and songs used in Israel's public worship. Several of these were originally battle hymns or victory hymns praising God. Considered among the oldest are the Song of Deborah in Judges 5, composed after the Israelites triumphed over the Canaanites at Taanach about 1125 B.C., and the Song of Miriam in Exodus 15, which may date from the Exodus from Egypt around 1280 B.C.

Some scholars think that the first community writing took place at Kadesh-barnea, the place the Israelites used as their main base during their years of wandering before they entered Canaan (Nm 13:26). Though Moses is not the actual author of the Pentateuch, the first five books of the Bible (his death is recorded in Deuteronomy 34:5), he is the inspiration behind it.

It is reasonable to think that he wrote down the basics of his teaching during this desert period.

Other early texts are blessings and oracles which cannot be clearly identified with any particular historical occasion. Examples are the boast of Lamech (Gn 4:23), the blessing of Rebekah (Gn 24:60), and the blessing of Isaac (Gn 27:27-29).

Monarchy. The Israelites entered the world of writing when David established his capital in Jerusalem. Official documents had to be kept in the same manner as they were kept by the surrounding nations. These documents dealt with history, trade, land transfer, international affairs, and military matters. A central storage place for official documents, or national archives, was required. We find references in the Bible to written historical sources used by the biblical writers such as the "Book of the Wars of the Lord" (Nm 21:14) and the "Book of Jashar" (Jos 10:13; 2 Sm 1:18-27).

David himself composed psalms and gave great impetus to the production of religious poetry and song. A talented writer in the time of David, drawing from his own eyewitness experience and using the various documents at his disposal, composed a colorful court history of the time. Part of this history is preserved in 2 Samuel 9-20 and 1 Kings 1-2. It traces how the royal crown passed from David to Solomon, in spite of intrigue, murder, and betrayal.

About the same time, perhaps during the reign of Solomon, another gifted author composed the first written account of Israel's development from the beginning. This writer is known as the "Yahwist" because he refers to God by the Hebrew name Yahweh not merely after the revelation of that divine name to Moses (Ex 3:14-15), but from the account of the creation itself.

There is no single biblical book which is said to have been written by this author, but much of the Pentateuch comes from his pen. We know now that his part of the Bible, which tells about the Creation and Fall, the ancestors of Israel, the Exodus, and the wandering, is the product of a complex process which took several centuries to complete. The Pentateuch received its final written form after the Exile in the fifth century before Christ. It is possible to see four major written sources or traditions that were woven together to produce a single narrative. They are called the "Yahwist," the "Elohist" (because of reference to God by the Hebrew name Elohim before the revelation of God's name to Moses in Exodus 3:14), the "Deuteronomist" (which includes Deuteronomy, with its stress on the need for reforms in social and religious law and justice), and the "Priestly" (which concentrates on rules about religious ritual, on religious covenants, and on genealogies).

The political unity and peace of the Israelite monarchy achieved under David gave the Yahwist and his contemporaries time to ponder the great religious questions: What kind of God is reponsible for saving us and bringing us to the land? Is he more powerful than the gods of other nations? If this God is good, where did evil come from? What is the connection between God and nature? The Yahwist looked back to the origins of humanity with the eyes of his Hebrew faith. He saw the God who had saved his people in the Exodus already preparing them long before they ever went to Egypt.

Divided Kingdom. Fifty to a hundred years after the Yahwist, the Elohist author wrote under very different conditions in the northern part of the divided kingdom (ninth century B.C.). The Elohist expressed his faith in the constant love of God by applying the idea of covenant to the relationship between God and his people. In the Pentateuch, the Elohist tradition begins with the covenant that God made with Abraham. The Elohist tradition often parallels the work of the Yahwist in the stories about the patriarchs and Moses. These two traditions (Yahwist and Elohist) were later combined by an unknown editor during the reign of King Hezekiah of Judah (2 Kgs 18–20), just about the time that the Deuteronomic and Priestly traditions were beginning to form.

During the ninth century before Christ, also, Elijah and his successor, Elisha, engaged in their prophetic work in the North (Israel). They were the first prophets to confront the king and national political and religious institutions (1 Kgs 16:29–19:18; 21; 2 Kgs 2–9; 13:14-21). This kind of moral and religious confrontation marks the prophets' role down through history. In the eighth century before Christ, the prophets Amos and Hosea spoke prophetic oracles which were the first to be written down. In the South (Judah) meantime, Isaiah of Jerusalem (Isaiah 1–39) and Micah of Moresheth (Micah) began their prophetic ministries. Because their disciples took notes, the tradition of writing down prophecy became well established.

Fall of Samaria. The intervention of foreigners into the national life of Israel and Judah profoundly affected the process by which the Bible was formed. This intervention would affect the Israelites for the next two hundred years. The first major disruption was the overthrow of Samaria, the royal city of Israel, by Assyria in 721 B.C. Many Israelites saw this event as the fulfillment of the warnings the prophets had made against the breakdown of moral standards and the mixture of pagan worship with the worship of God. Priests who had descended from Levi and had been active at the northern sanctuaries escaped to Judah. They preserved the distinctive religious traditions of Israel. Their own experience prepared them well to support King Hezekiah's plan to destroy the places of Baal worship and to reform worship as it was practiced in the Jerusalem Temple and to centralize worship there.

The teaching of these northern priests would have far-reaching influence on the composition of the Bible. It became the core of the Deuteronomic tradition, which is found in the Book of Deuteronomy, and is the work of the Deuteronomic historians who edited Joshua, Judges, 1 and 2 Samuel, and 1 and 2 Kings. This tradition insisted on a central sanctuary and on moral and religious reform. It also spoke warmly of God's love for his people and of their free choice to enter into a covenantal relationship with him. This tradition also emphasized the present reality of this covenant in their lives.

The reform of Hezekiah, however, was not destined to endure. His son, Manasseh, has been called the worst king in Judah's history. He overturned the policy of the single sanctuary dedicated to God, and he encouraged the worship of false gods in the fertility cults of the "high places" on the hilltops (2 Kgs 21:1-18). Manasseh's son Amon followed in his father's footsteps (2 Kgs 21:19-26).

Josiah's Reform. A new burst of religious enthusiasm and literary activity came with the reign of Josiah. Prompted by the "people of the land" (2 Kgs 21:24), who were disgusted with the direction that the royal court had taken under Manasseh and Amon, Josiah repudiated the foreign gods of his father and grandfather. Then in 621 B.C., when the high priest Hilkiah found the "Book of the Law" in the Temple, Josiah inaugurated a full-scale religious reform. The scroll discovered by Hilkiah seems to have been the Deuteronomic Code (Dt 12–26) written during the time of Hezekiah and set aside under Manasseh and Amon.

Several prophets proclaimed the divine message during this period (there are written records, for example, from Zephaniah, Nahum, and Habakkuk), but the great spokesman of the time was Jeremiah. He received his call in 627 B.C. during Josiah's early years, and was Israel's conscience until the exile in 587 B.C. Jeremiah's secretary, Baruch, preserved much of Jeremiah's speaking and writing on the eve of the deportation of the people to Babylon.

Babylonian Exile. In 587 B.C. the disaster which Jeremiah had been predicting came to pass. The Babylonian king, Nebuchadnezzar, destroyed Jerusalem and led the people into exile. This dark period of Israelite history turned out to be a particularly fruitful period of sacred writing. Although the exiles were isolated from the Temple, they kept alive the old prayers and songs (Ps 137). The psalter contains several new compositions from this period. In Jerusalem, meanwhile, some of the few who had not been deported wept over the ruins and the emptiness of the city. Their sorrow eventually produced the plaintive Lamentations. Priests in exile devoted themselves to collecting old traditions from the days of the desert wanderings and to setting down in order an account of the practices of worship in the days when the Temple was the center of worship in Jerusalem. Two prophets, Ezekiel and Second Isaiah (Isaiah 40–55), gave new hope with oracles that proclaimed that one day the exiles would return and restore the nations. When the Israelites emerged from the exile, they brought the core of the Hebrew Scriptures with them.

Restoration. The return to Jerusalem in 538 B.C. was not as glorious as the exiles had dreamed it would be. Tensions involved in rebuilding the city and the Temple are revealed in the writings of Haggai and Zechariah 1 (Zechariah 1-8); a more thorough story is told in the books of Ezra and Nehemiah, which, along with 1 and 2 Chronicles, show how the anonymous author we call the Chronicler understood history as the working out of God's will.

The priests continued their important editing work. Sometime in the fifth century these authors, whom we call all together "the Priestly tradition," put the Pentateuch into its final form. The Book of Deuteronomy, which for awhile had served as the introduction to the history continued in the books from Joshua through Kings, now became the concluding book of the Pentateuch. The writing of prophetic literature gradually declined during the fifth and fourth centuries. There were visions of the future in promises of a perfect messianic sacrifice (Malachi), and a great Day of the Lord (Joel, Zechariah 9-14); and glances to the past as in Obadiah's cry for vengeance against the Edomites. The Book of Ruth was also written during this time, as was Jonah, which, though listed with the prophetic books, is a satire on Judah's narrow nationalism.

Wisdom Literature. The largest single block of biblical writing associated with postexilic Judah is the group of books belonging to the wisdom tradition: Job, Psalms, Proverbs, Ecclesiastes, Song of Songs, Sirach (Ecclesiasticus), and Wisdom. "Wisdom literature" is a broad category. It originated outside Israel in the court life of neighboring nations, particularly Egypt, and is full of instructive "words for wise living." These short, pointed sayings are found especially in Proverbs and Sirach. Wisdom literature also contains a collection of marriage songs (Song of Songs), a poetic masterpiece on the mystery of suffering (Job), and a meditation on the mystery of life itself (Ecclesiastes, also called Qoheleth).

The wisdom literature of Israel is linked with the name of King Solomon, though little of it can actually go back to his time. He was famous as "the wisest of men"; and in the ancient world, books were often said to be written by great leaders in order to make sure that they survived and were circulated. Thus Ecclesiastes, Song of Songs, and Wisdom, all written after Israel returned from the Exile, were presented as though they had been written by Solomon. In the same way, Moses was given credit for writing the Pentateuch, and David the Psalms.

A new set of influences began to affect Judah after Alexander the Great conquered Syria and Palestine in 333 B.C. Greek ways became a threat to the worship of God in the traditional manner, just as Baal worship had been in earlier times. Biblical writings of the period contain warnings against adopting Greek lifestyles. Hellenizing—the adoption of Greek culture—remained subtle until the Syrian ruler, Antiochus IV Epiphanes, came to the throne. He was determined to crush the worship of Israel's God.

Severe religious persecution provoked the Maccabean revolt of 167-164 B.C., described by two different historians fifty to seventy-five years later (1 and 2 Maccabees). The Book of Daniel was published during the years of persecution to encourage hope and faithfulness. Daniel uses a form of language and imagery called "apocalyptic." It concentrates on the "last days" of judgment and final victory. It makes its point by telling stories of beasts, of battles in the heavens, and of dreams and visions. Most of this book is written in Hebrew; but part of it, for an unknown reason, is in Aramaic. (A section of the Book of Ezra is also in Aramaic.) Other late Old Testament productions were in the "historical novel" tradition: Esther, Tobit, and Judith.

Old Testament Canon. The Old Testament took a long time to develop. None of the authors thought of themselves as composing divinely inspired literature which would be used as a guide by succeeding generations. The prophets understood their spoken utterances as coming from God, but the written records of prophecy came only gradually to share such authority.

How did an authorized collection of inspired writings develop in Israel? This is the question of the "canon," from the Greek term for rod or cane, which eventually became the word for "norm" or "standard." The first step in the canonizing process was the finding of the Deuteronomic Code in the Temple in 621 B.C. Because it was thought to have been written by Moses, this book became the unquestioned word from God to guide King Josiah's reform. For the first time a writing was officially recognized as the word of God. Over the next two hundred years other writings expanded the law given through Moses, including the narrative accounts of Israel's origins. By 400 B.C., the different strands of material had become the five books of the Pentateuch, which was published at this time as the *Torah,* or Law, and was accepted as the written word of God.

Meanwhile the Deuteronomic history of Joshua, Judges, Samuel, and Kings continued to enjoy popularity and grew in stature as a definitive record. Some of the prophetic collections were appearing: Isaiah, Jeremiah, Ezekiel, and the minor prophets. As the Jewish community used these books, they recognized their authentic message of faith. By 200 B.C. these books came to be generally accepted as the part of the Bible called the "Prophets."

The wisdom literature and other books from the postexilic period were referred to as the "Writings," a convenient catchall title for works not contained in the Law or the Prophets. At the time of Jesus there were still disputes over the canonicity of some of these books. Those disputes continue to have their influence, as witnessed by the differences among Catholics, Orthodox, Protestants, various eastern Christians, and Jews about the number of books in the Old Testament. This issue will be dealt with in the following chapter.

New Testament

The formation of the New Testament was a process comparable to the development of the Old Testament. Jesus left no written records. His Bible and that quoted by his disciples was the Old Testament. The first complete Christian document dates from twenty years after his lifetime (1 Thessalonians); and it was another twenty years or so before a Gospel (Mark) appeared. The New Testament literature, like that of the Old Testament, emerged within the community of believers according to their own needs and the guidance of the Spirit as they reflected on and responded to the drama of salvation in Christ.

In the first years after the Resurrection, there was little thought given to producing and collecting Christian writings. Some of this was undoubtedly due to the example of the Lord himself who, like the rabbis of the time, taught by the spoken word, which in turn was remembered and discussed by disciples. There was no need for writing while the apostles were still alive to clarify or verify anything uncertain. Because his followers expected Jesus to return soon, any permanent writing of his teaching seemed unnecessary, and perhaps faithless.

There was, however, some writing going on in the Christian community in the earliest decades. As in Israel, the Christian liturgy among predominantly Jewish or gentile groups was a mixture of songs, creeds, psalms, and other prayers (Col 3:16). Paul's writings contain excerpts from these sources (for example, the hymns in Philippians 2:6-11 and Colossians 1:15-20). Sayings of Jesus were being collected between A.D. 30 and 40. Eventually these formed a chain of episodes, probably appearing first in the Aramaic language, then in Greek. Parts of this document, now called "Q" from the German *Quelle,* "source," are traceable in Matthew and Luke. In addition to "Q," other collections may have been used by preachers: collections of parables, prooftexts from the Scriptures, and notes on various deeds of Jesus. An early account of the Passion was also written.

Paul. The first unified Christian writings to come down to us are the letters of Paul. They were attempts to bridge the distances as the apostle traveled from community to community in Asia Minor (present-day Turkey) and Greece. Even in the earliest of these letters, 1 and 2 Thessalonians (A.D. 50-51), he wrote with a pattern of encouragement, correction, and instruction which he later used in all his letters. Paul's major doctrinal work appeared in the middle 50s: Galatians, 1 and 2 Corinthians, and Romans. The Captivity Letters (Philippians, Philemon, Colossians, and Ephesians) were written while Paul was in prison at various times in Caesarea, Ephesus, or Rome. Philippians, the most affectionate of Paul's letters, is the first of this group. Ephesians is the last, and differences in style and vocabulary from Paul's earlier letters make his authorship of this letter questionable. Since it is not addressed to any particular community ("To the Ephesians" is a note added later), this letter may have been composed by one of Paul's disciples as a summary of Paul's doctrine to be circulated among the churches in Asia Minor.

The Pastoral Letters (1 and 2 Timothy, Titus) give attention to the new situations that arose when Christian communities became more settled and were more formally organized. The letter to the Hebrews, long thought to be written by Paul, is now recognized as the work of a later disciple. It presents an interpretation of Christ's priesthood which is unique in the New Testament.

The Gospels. As Paul neared the end of his ministry, the writing of the four Gospels began. Because they appear first in order among New Testament books and because they tell the story of Jesus, we tend to think that the Gospels were the first Christian documents written. As we have seen, Paul's letters were the first Christian writings. In fact, Paul himself probably died before the first Gospel, Mark, was in circulation.

The memory of Jesus' words and deeds was kept alive by preachers and storytellers in the various Christian communities. However, the accounts of Jesus differed slightly from community to community. A story was told with a different emphasis at Rome than at Jerusalem or Ephesus; Alexandria remembered incidents that had never been heard of at Corinth. Christians feared that some important material or the meaning of it would be lost. New converts asked for a systematic presentation of the story of Jesus.

Mark. The Gospel of Mark appeared around A.D. 70, not long after the martyrdom of the great leaders, Peter, Paul, and James of Jerusalem. It is difficult for us to appreciate the achievement that the writing of the first Gospel represents. Mark had to compose something for new Christians and for prospective converts that would tell the basic story, but not be too lengthy or heavy for the interested reader. By this time, inaccuracy and rumor clouded the information about Jesus' life and teaching. Theories about the meaning of God's saving act in Jesus needed to be sorted out and evaluated. As far as we know, Mark was the first writer of a life of Jesus, so he could not compare his work with that of others.

The story he told became a source of material for other Gospel writers to follow. It became the standard by which they evaluated information about Jesus. Mark's Gospel is not exactly a biography of Jesus; many questions about Jesus' life are left unanswered. Nor is it merely a catechism, nor a sermon about the meaning of Jesus. But in a way it is all these things. The essentials of Jesus' life and teaching are presented and interpreted simply and clearly. But Mark does not get wound up in details. He does not recite everything that Jesus did; he records little of the preaching. He keeps the eyes of the reader on the person of Jesus, the Christ, the Son of God.

Matthew. Mark's Gospel probably originated in Rome. Non-Jewish Christians were its primary audience. The need for a Gospel written primarily for Jewish Christians developed. After the destruction of Jerusalem and its Temple in A.D. 70, the Jewish community closed ranks behind the leadership of the rabbis. They saw the rise of Christianity as a challenge to their own religious traditions and identity. Some may have associated Christianity with the Roman threat.

This led to laws banning Christians from the synagogues and to other separations, arousing much confusion and some bitterness on the part of Christian converts from Judaism. They felt alienated from their families. In some cases, they were cut off and even disowned. Up to this time many still thought of themselves as Jews, but Jews who had discovered the full meaning and completion of the ancient promises. Even the apostles continued to worship as Jews for a time (Acts 3:1). Now it seemed that the family and religious roots of Jewish Christians were severed.

The Gospel of Matthew was written for these Jewish Christians in Palestine and Syria about A.D. 85. There is a tradition of a gospel written in Aramaic much earlier by the apostle Matthew, but the Gospel of Matthew in our Bibles was written by a later disciple in Greek. Though Matthew used Mark's Gospel as his framework, his work is almost twice as long as Mark's. Much of the additional material comes out of his concern that Jewish converts should understand Jesus' mission and their Christian faith as the fulfillment of the Old Testament promises. Matthew quotes the Old Testament Scriptures more than sixty times.

Luke and Acts. At about the same time that Matthew wrote his Gospel, a Greek Christian convert of Asia Minor composed a two-volume story of Jesus and the early Church. The Gospel of Luke and the Acts of the Apostles were directed to the Greek-speaking communities of the Roman empire. Their concerns and needs were different from those of the Jewish converts of Matthew's community. Luke's readers did not need reassurance about the Old Testament (which they had probably never read), but they needed to know how their own Christian faith, which had come to them through missionary preachers, was based on the words and deeds of Jesus. They probably wondered about the Jewish traditions of the liturgy and asked about the Jewish origins of their faith. They would have been interested in knowing how a Jewish religion had become open to all people.

John. The Gospel of John was the last of the four Gospels. It probably originated in Asia Minor, near Ephesus, in the last decade of the first century. It contains practically no repetition (except in the Passion account) of material covered in the earlier gospels. John's Gospel grew out of a Christian community which looked to the "disciple whom Jesus loved" (Jn 13:23), the "beloved disciple," as their founder and which strongly identified Jesus as the Son of God. He is the Word who "became flesh" (1:14) and the "bread of life" (6:35) for his followers.

The three letters of John, written a few years later, had to counteract extravagant notions of Jesus' divinity. False teachers were saying that Jesus only seemed to be human. The first letter is a beautiful essay on the love of God revealed in Jesus; the other two present particular messages for local communities.

Catholic Epistles and Revelation. The New Testament letters outside the Pauline collection are often grouped together under the heading "Catholic Epistles," those addressed to the whole Church instead of to a particular community. James' letter is an example of New Testament wisdom literature. It applies the gospel message to practical issues of Christian morality. First Peter is also concerned with the practice of the faith, but with much more emphasis on the doctrinal basis for Christian behavior. Some of its beautiful and memorable passages seem to have been influenced by an early baptismal liturgy. Jude and 2 Peter were both written to combat errors that emerged in the last part of the first century.

The last book in the Bible is in a category by itself. It is known as the Revelation, or the Apocalypse. The apocalyptic form of writing was used in the Old Testament (in books such as Ezekiel and Daniel) and in several apocryphal books (see chapter 8) written before A.D. 200. In Daniel and Revelation, this form was used for crisis literature: that is, books written to strengthen the faith and hope of a community in the midst of persecution and suffering. The occasion of Daniel was the persecution of the Jewish community by Antiochus IV Epiphanes; for Revelation, it was the Roman persecution of Christians.

New Testament Canon. Compared to the long process of canonization of the Old Testament books, acceptance of the writings of the apostles and Gospel writers as inspired Scripture came quickly. Reference to New Testament books as the standard for faith and practice are found in writings as early as those by Clement of Rome and Ignatius of Antioch at the beginning of the second century. Tertullian, about A.D. 200, is the first to use the title "New Testament." The canonization process was hastened as a result of the rejection of the Old Testament and most of the New Testament by the Christian heretic, Marcion, about A.D. 150. Disputes continued about whether the New Testament should include the books of Hebrews, James, 2 Peter, 2 and 3 John, and Revelation. On the other hand, some books no longer in the canon were considered inspired at different times. These were *1 and 2 Clement*, the *Didache*, and the

Shepherd of Hermas. It was not until the fourth century that the New Testament canon was finally fixed.

How were the present New Testament books finally selected? Various factors were considered: apostolic origin, the importance of the community addressed, the centrality of the doctrine contained. In the final analysis, however, it was the Church's awareness, under the guidance of the Holy Spirit, that certain books were an authentic and necessary reflection of her own life of faith. The community of believers saw its own faith mirrored in these books. These books have been the primary standard of Christian faith ever since.

FOUR

Why There Are Different Christian Bibles

Arguments about the makeup of the Bible are a puzzle to believers and unbelievers alike. Are there sixty-six books in the Bible, as the Protestants say, or seventy-three, as the Catholics say? How can Christians be split on this central question about the written word of God? As noted in the preceding chapter, the difficulty lies in the Old Testament. Almost all Christians accept the same twenty-seven New Testament books. But besides the thirty-nine books revered as inspired by Protestant Christians (and Jews), Catholics include seven additional books: Baruch, Judith, 1 and 2 Maccabees, Sirach (Ecclesiasticus), Tobit, and Wisdom; as well as expanded versions of the books of Daniel and Esther. These books are known by Catholics as the "Deuterocanonicals" and by Protestants as "The Apocrypha," terms which will be explained later.

The mention of the Jews reminds us that this is not exclusively, and was not originally, a Christian debate. The current differences among Christians stem from the unsettled state of the Jewish scriptural canon in the early days of the Church. A final decision on the contents of the Old Testament was not made in Judaism until the second or third century after Christ.

This does not mean that the Jews did not have a "Bible" of inspired writings before that time. As we have seen, the group of books known as the "Torah" was accepted as the word of

God by 400 B.C., and the "Prophets" by 200 B.C. (Note the reference to the Twelve Minor Prophets as a group by Jesus ben Sirach, writing probably between 200 and 175 B.C.: Sir 49:10). But the canonicity of a later group of books known as the "Writings" remained unsettled for many years. The writings were used in teaching and eventually in the liturgy by various Jewish communities, but there was no pressure to decide which of them should be ranked on a level with the Torah and Prophets. That the rabbis finally did establish a definitive collection owed less to the internal needs of Judaism than to pressure from the outside: Christians had begun quoting some of the disputed books as Scripture and were implicitly canonizing writings which belonged to the Jews.

Language, cultural developments, and geography gave rise to the differences of opinion in the Jewish community. The Jews had begun to lose their homogeneous language and culture by the time of the deportations into Mesopotamia by the Assyrians and Babylonians (eighth, seventh, and sixth centuries B.C.) and the early migrations to Egypt (sixth century B.C.). During the ascendancy of the Persians in the ancient Near East (547-333 B.C.), Aramaic, a related Semitic tongue, replaced Hebrew as the language of the common people. Many Jews could no longer read the Scriptures in Hebrew, which prompted the production of Aramaic translations ("targums," from the Aramaic word for translation) for use in the synagogues.

Hellenism

Alexander the Great ended Persian rule at the battle of Issus (present-day Turkey) in 333 B.C. He established Greek rule and cultural influence by setting up a series of military colonies and founding Greek-style cities, the most important of these being Alexandria (331 B.C.) in Egypt. The Greek language and way of life began to penetrate the eastern Mediterranean world.

The diffusion of Greek civilization is known as Hellenism (from "Hellas," Greece). There was a two-way exchange: the subjected peoples adopted the Greek language as the common *(koine)* tongue and accepted many other Greek influences, and the classical features of Greek language and culture were modified by contact with the Mediterranean world. The Jews, in spite of the tenacity of their own religious and cultural traditions, were also affected by this Hellenistic movement, particularly those scattered beyond the confines of Palestine. Jewish leaders feared that the younger generation would lose the common faith through adaptation to the new cultural wave. This was not idle speculation, as we know from the Books of Maccabees (1 Mc 1:11-15; 2 Mc 4:7-17). Antiochus IV Epiphanes (175-164 B.C.) made a concerted attempt to eradicate the Jewish faith (1 Mc 1:41-50), prompting the Maccabean revolt (167-164 B.C.) which successfully stemmed the tide of religious decline.

Nevertheless Hellenism continued. Already in the third century B.C., the Hebrew Scriptures had become inaccessible to many Jews in the Greek-speaking empire. A Greek translation of the biblical books appeared in Alexandria around 200 B.C. This became known as the Septuagint (from the Latin for "seventy"), because of the legend that the translation had been done by seventy-two translators, six from each of the twelve tribes. The Septuagint became the Bible of the Jews of the "Diaspora" (those "dispersed" in foreign lands). It was later adopted by the Christian missionaries when they took the gospel into the Hellenistic world of the Roman empire. The New Testament, written in Greek, records 300 of its 350 quotations from the Septuagint version of the Old Testament instead of in direct translation from the Hebrew.

The Septuagint translation was written during the period when the validity of the "Writings" was still in question. Besides the Torah and Prophets, the Greek translators included other religious books used in synagogue worship, such as Proverbs and the Song of Songs. Recent textual investigation shows that the Septuagint was not translated all at once but over a period of time and by different individuals or groups. But by the first century of the present era it had achieved widespread circulation and authority in the Greek-speaking Jewish world. By this time also, more recent Jewish books used in teaching and worship had become part of the Septuagint. Some of these are the books now disputed among Protestants, Catholics, and Jews: books written in Greek (Judith, 2 Maccabees, Wisdom, Baruch) or written in Hebrew (1 Maccabees, Sirach) or Aramaic (Tobit) and translated into Greek. Two other books produced during the same period (after 200 B.C.) appear as inspired writings in all Jewish and Christian Bibles (Daniel, Esther). But only Catholic Bibles treat them as inspired books in their longer form, as they appear in the Septuagint. All of these books circulated among the Greek-speaking Jews as Scripture for many years, including all during the lifetime of Jesus. Debate about their canonicity arose later.

Different Canonical Traditions

While the Septuagint became the Jewish Bible of the Greek-speaking Mediterranean world, in Palestine the Hebrew Bible remained the standard. The Palestinian collection did not contain some of the books used at Alexandria, but there was no concern about a uniform edition. Jews used the writings which met the needs of their local communities. All of these books, Hebrew or Greek or Aramaic in origin, were considered part of the sacred writings, though usually the books among the Writings were not treated with the same reverence accorded the Torah.

I have already mentioned that a final decision on the canon of the Jewish Bible was not made until the second or third century A.D. But the first step in this process took place during the last part of the first century in a Jewish reaction to Christianity. The first Christians were observant Jews. Jesus was a regular worshiper in the Temple and the synagogue (Lk 4:16), and so were his followers. In the early Church, Christians considered themselves the true Jews who understood the fulfillment of God's promises; they participated in the Temple liturgy and celebrated the Eucharist at home (Acts 2:46). They continued to use the Jewish Scriptures as their Bible.

After the fall of Jerusalem and the destruction of the Temple by the Romans (A.D. 70), suspicion about the Christian Jews and their true allegiances intensified in the Jewish community. The rabbis were the new leaders now that there was no Temple for a priesthood. They gathered at Jamnia (Jabneh), a city west of Jerusalem near the Mediterranean Sea, to establish a center for building up the battered Jewish nation and religion. Before the tragedy of A.D. 70, Judaism embraced many diverse elements

(Pharisees, Sadducees, Zealots, Essenes, Christians). The rabbis felt that this diversity had brought about harmful divisions, sapping Jewish loyalties and orthodoxy, and contributing to the downfall of the nation. They sought to eliminate all divisive elements by establishing a strict orthodoxy.

The Jewish Christians were identified as unorthodox and were forced to choose between Judaism and Christianity. The hostilities of this period (late first century) are reflected in the Gospels of Matthew and John written during this time. Families were split over their allegiances to the synagogue or the Church; Jesus' predictions took on vivid meaning (Mt 10:34-37).

The Bible was fundamental to the Jewish religion and to the rabbis' reform. Jamnia became famous for its school of Torah study. The rabbis were called on to interpret the Law throughout the Jewish community. For a long time it was thought that the Jamnia rabbis were the authorities who established the (shorter) Old Testament canon now used by Jews in reaction to Christian use of a wider selection. But recent studies cast doubt on this supposition. Evidence shows that debates took place at Jamnia over the canonicity of Ecclesiastes and the Song of Songs (both of which are now accepted as part of the Hebrew Bible), but there is no evidence that they outlawed the deuterocanonical books. In fact, one of the disputed books, Sirach, was still being read and copied by the Jews after the Jamnia period.

No Explicit Canon

During the formative days of the Christian Church, the Jews did not possess a formal or explicit canon of Old Testament books. The Christian writers quoted the broad library of sacred writings used among contemporary Jews. The Jews continued their own discussions about the sacred books, and in the late second or early third century canonized the shorter collection that Jews and Protestants use today. Modern study by all parties to the current debate have raised questions about the correctness of this late Jewish decision to exclude some of the books which had been accepted as Scripture for more than two hundred years.

The Christians did not establish their Old Testament canon as early as the Jews. Apparently, they did not consider the question of great importance to the Church, and continued to use the writings included in the Septuagint as before. Christian attention was probably diverted by the far more crucial question of the contents of the New Testament canon.

Christians began establishing their own library of sacred writings by the end of the first century (see chapter 3). Meanwhile, Christian use of the Old Testament went on as before. In the third century, after the Jewish canonical decision, the Christian writer Origen was aware that the Jews had a shorter canon than that customarily used in the Church. In the fourth century, St. Athanasius, who was instructed by Jewish teachers, made a strong appeal for the acceptance of the shorter canon by the Church. Not long after his time, St. Jerome began translating the whole Bible into Latin. He sought out Jewish scholars to teach him Hebrew, and was soon proposing also that the Church adopt the Old Testament canon of the Jews. But neither Athanasius nor Jerome was able to influence Church usage or the North African councils at Hippo and Carthage (late fourth century) which accepted a longer Old Testament canon. In fact, Jerome's Latin translation (the "Vulgate," or common-language, version) which became the standard Christian Bible in the western Church, contains the longer canon.

The Reformation

The question of the Old Testament canon rested during the next thousand years until it was raised again by the Reformers in the sixteenth century. In his translation of 1534, Martin Luther grouped the deuterocanonical books together at the end of the Old Testament as books which "are not held equal to the sacred Scriptures and yet are useful and good for reading." The Reformers, in deciding to get back to the situation at the time of the Church's origin, wanted to adopt as Scripture the books that had made up the Old Testament used by the early Christians. They presumed that the books revered by the Jews in the sixteenth century had always been the canonical Old Testament, and so the shorter list of books became the Old Testament of the Reformers. They did not know that the decision for a shorter Old Testament canon had been late in coming, and that during the first century both Jews and Christians held a wider selection of Old Testament books. In response to the Reformers, the Council of Trent in 1546 defined the longer Old Testament canon as inspired Scripture.

Today

In our modern ecumenical climate, the dispute about the deuterocanonicals has dissipated. Protestants have returned to the practice of the earliest days of the Reformation in publishing the disputed books along with the other biblical books, but in a separate section. Protestant and Catholic scholars are reexamining the history of the formation of the canon, and studying the debate between the Reformers and the Council of Trent.

"Deuterocanonical" is the Catholic term for the disputed Old Testament books. "Deutero" is Greek for "second," and "deuterocanonical" indicates that these books were accepted into the Bible after the "protocanonical" (first-canonical) books had already been approved. Protestants call these books the "apocrypha" (from the Greek word for "hidden"). To complicate terminology even more, there is a body of ancient Jewish writings which neither Protestants nor Catholics consider inspired. The Protestant name for them is "pseudepigrapha" ("false writings"), but Catholics call them the "apocrypha."

Bible Translations

A related question in the area of Bible variations, but on a different level, is the issue of Bible translations. Until about 1940, English-speaking Catholics and Protestants were easily distinguishable by the Bibles they used. Catholics all used the Douay-Rheims Bible, the translation from the Latin Vulgate made by English Catholic exiles on the European continent (1582-1609), in the revision prepared by Bishop Richard Challoner

(1763). Most Protestants used the Authorized, or "King James," Version, translated from the original languages and published by a commission of British scholars appointed by James I (1611), either in its original form or in the Revised Version of England (1885) or the American Standard Version (1901).

Now a broad range of English Bible translations is available, and Catholics and Protestants no longer feel limited to the use of their "own" Bibles. Some modern translations are no longer in vogue, either among Catholics (Knox, Westminster, Kleist-Lilly) or Protestants (Moffat, Goodspeed, Phillips). The most popular and influential English versions are known by their initials as KJV, RSV and NRSV, NAB, NIV, JB and NJB, NEB and REB, and GNB. They will be examined individually in this chapter, along with a paraphrase (LB) and a digest (RDB).

Types of Translation

Scholars speak of two ways of translating the Bible: the formal equivalence method and the dynamic equivalence method. In formal equivalence, the translator tries to match word for word and phrase for phrase as closely as possible while still making the text readable. In dynamic equivalence, the translator is not concerned about matching words so much as matching thoughts. The translation gives meaning for meaning instead of word for word. For example, a formal equivalence translation of Genesis 1:24 is: "And God said, 'Let the earth bring forth living creatures according to their kinds: cattle and creeping things and beasts of the earth according to their kinds.' And it was so" (RSV). In a dynamic equivalence translation this is: "Then God commanded, 'Let the earth produce all kinds of animal life: domestic and wild, large and small'—and it was done" (GNB).

The first example is rather solemn, though not archaic. The second sounds more like modern English. In general, a formal equivalence translation is better for study, a dynamic equivalence translation may be better for personal and public reading. When there are ambiguities in the original text, a formal equivalence translator will reproduce them in the translation. This can be frustrating for ordinary reading, but helpful to the student who wants to be aware of problems in the text. A dynamic equivalence translator will solve the ambiguity by making a decision about the meaning to be conveyed.

These distinctions between the two methods are not always clear. All translators are concerned about delivering the true meaning of the text in clear and readable language, and translation is an unremitting series of decisions. Among the modern English translations most used today, three fall into the formal equivalence category: the Revised Standard Version and the New Revised Standard Version (RSV/NRSV), the New American Bible (NAB), and the New International Version (NIV). Four employ dynamic equivalence: the Jerusalem Bible and the New Jerusalem Bible (JB/NJB), the New English Bible and the Revised English Bible (NEB/REB), the Good News Bible (GNB), and the Contemporary English Version (CEV).

Revised Standard Version (1952); **New Revised Standard Version** (1991). The RSV has the reputation among English translations of being the closest in wording to the original languages. Therefore it, and its revision, the NRSV, are the favorites for Scripture classes in seminaries and universities. The RSV is the modern heir of the King James tradition. KJV was the Bible of the Protestant English-speaking world for almost three hundred years before the discovery of more ancient biblical manuscripts and the archaisms of the language prompted a revision. In 1885, British scholars published the Revised Version (RV), which was adapted for the United States in 1901 as the American Standard Version (ASV).

The RSV was commissioned as a thorough revision of the ASV by the National Council of Churches in 1937. The New Testament appeared in 1946, the Old Testament in 1952, and the Apocrypha (deuterocanonicals) in 1956. Editions entitled *The Revised Standard Version with the Apocrypha* include all the biblical books used by Catholics: this translation was approved for Catholic use by the *imprimatur* of Cardinal Richard Cushing in 1965. *The Oxford Annotated Bible,* with or without the Apocrypha, is the RSV with footnotes. The 1977 edition of the *Oxford Annotated,* which was issued as an "ecumenical study Bible," did away with mention of "Protestant" or "Catholic" books and "Apocrypha" and simply included "all the books accepted as authoritative by all the branches of the Christian Church."

In 1991, a New Revised Standard Version (NRSV) with the Apocrypha was published. Besides reflecting textual research since 1952, the NRSV makes new decisions in passages where masculine pronouns were used in the RSV. The new revision also eliminated remaining archaisms, such as *thee, thou, and behold.*

In 2000, St. Mary's Press brought out the Catholic Youth Bible, a study Bible designed for young people. This offers a great deal of explanatory material in small blocks spread throughout the biblical text. Not only high school students but many adults would find it helpful.

New American Bible (1970); Revised New Testament (1986); Revised Psalms (1991). The NAB has become the most widely used Bible among American Catholics in the post-Vatican II era. This is due in part to its production and promotion under official Church auspices and its connection with Catholic liturgy. But the particular balance and blend of approaches have given the translation its own popularity. It is literal enough to reflect the style of the original languages (particularly the Hebrew), but generally free enough in expression to be readable and understandable. The New Testament was revised in 1986. The Psalms were revised in 1991.

The Douay-Rheims-Challoner Bible was the counterpart for English-speaking Catholics of the King James Bible through three centuries. In the late 1930s, the American bishops authorized a revision of the New Testament under the direction of the Committee for the Confraternity of Christian Doctrine. This CCD New Testament, which appeared in 1941, was still based on the Latin Vulgate as required by the Council of Trent. A revision of the Old Testament was cancelled when, in 1943, Pope Pius XII in his encyclical *Divino Afflante Spiritu* encouraged translations of the Bible from the original languages. A completely new translation of the Old Testament from Hebrew, Aramaic, and Greek appeared in segments beginning in 1948. A provisional translation of New Testament passages from the Greek was used in the English Mass when the vernacular readings were first allowed in 1964. The translations of both Old and New Testaments went on until the publication of the finished product, the NAB, in 1970.

There are two major Catholic study Bibles which use the NRSV, both from Oxford University Press: The Catholic Study Bible (1990) and the Catholic Bible: Personal Study Edition

(1995). Both of these provide hundreds of pages of supplementary articles and background information in a section before the biblical text. The Catholic Bible: Personal Study Edition also includes questions for reflection.

New International Version (1978). This American translation received its impetus in the hostile reaction of many conservative Protestants to the RSV. They feared that in adopting a more critical text (selecting different manuscripts as the basis for the translation) and in dropping time-honored phrases from KJV, the translators had tampered with essentials. The dissatisfaction simmered until 1965, when a group of scholars meeting in Chicago decided to produce a new critical translation to compete with the RSV.

The result is a good critical translation, not quite as literal as the RSV and without the "thee's" and "thou's" and other archaisms. In this regard it is more liberal than the original RSV. Daniel Harrington, S.J., notes the irony that "the translation inspired to some extent by suspicions about the theological orthodoxy of the RSV should end up being quite close to the RSV" (*Interpreting the Old Testament*). The NIV does not include the deuterocanonical books of the Old Testament recognized by Catholics as part of the canon of Scripture.

Jerusalem Bible (1966); **New Jerusalem Bible** (1985). While American Catholic scholars were responding to *Divino Afflante Spiritu* with the translations which would become the NAB, French Dominican scholars at the Ecole Biblique in Jerusalem were producing the Jerusalem Bible, a dynamic equivalence translation with extensive introductions, notes, and cross-references. The complete French edition appeared in 1956, the English edition in 1966. The JB attained immediate popularity as the first complete Bible in easy-reading English for Catholics. Its excellent notes made this Bible a great source of instruction.

Strangely, though the JB avoided literalism to the point of paraphrase at times, it took the unprecedented step of using "Yahweh" for God's name in the Old Testament, a transliteration of the Hebrew. The Jewish-Christian tradition had avoided using this name because of the ancient Jewish reverence which prohibited its utterance. The use of "Yahweh" in JB produced some ecumenical ripples.

A new edition of the JB appeared in French in 1973; and in English in 1985.

New English Bible (1971); **Revised English Bible** (1989). About the time the New Testament translation of the RSV appeared (1946), the General Assembly of the Church of Scotland called for a new English translation which would break away from the "Bible English" used in the KJV-RV-ASV-RSV tradition. In their statement of purpose for the rendering of the New Testament, the translators presented a clear description of the dynamic equivalence method: "We have conceived our task to be that of understanding the original as precisely as we could (using all available aids), and then saying again in our own native idiom what we believed the author to be saying in his. We have found that in practice this frequently compelled us to make decisions where the older method of translation allowed a comfortable ambiguity." NEB became noted for the high quality of its language.

A revision of the NEB appeared in 1989 under the name Revised English Bible.

Good News Bible (1979). GNB (also known as Today's English Version—TEV) is a dynamic equivalence translation produced by the American Bible Society, which for over a century and a half has been disseminating the Bible to people all over the world in easily understandable translations.

Because a translation like this has to be readable for people of various English-speaking traditions as well as for people for whom English is a second language, the sentence structure has been kept simple and the vocabulary limited. Such a procedure carries the risk of falsifying the text or producing flat, colorless English. But careful scholarship aided the decisions. Footnotes indicate the other options where a significant choice of text or translation has been made. And the translation is clear, bright, and lively. A special feature is the simple line drawings included throughout to illustrate the text.

The New Testament appeared in 1966 with the title *Good News for Modern Man.* The Bible without the deuterocanonical books was published ten years later, and the complete Bible, *the Good News Bible with Deuterocanonicals/Apocrypha,* appeared in 1979.

Contemporary English Version (1995). The American Bible Society noticed a need for fresh translation of Scripture that would be suited for reading aloud and would be easily comprehensible when heard. After several years of work, the ABS brought out the CEV, which is a dynamic-equivalence rendering of the biblical text marked by simplicity, clarity, ease of comprehension, and, in the poetic sections, an elegant economy of expression.

Translation Samples

To give the reader a taste of the different approaches to text by the Bibles reviewed above, here are their translations of a familiar New Testament passage, the dialogue between Jesus and the father of the boy with an evil spirit in Mark 9:23-24.

RSV: "And Jesus said to him ... 'All things are possible to him who believes.' Immediately the father of the child cried out and said, 'I believe; help my unbelief!'"

NAB: "Jesus said to him ... 'Everything is possible to one who has faith.' Then the boy's father cried out, 'I do believe, help my unbelief!'"

NIV: "...'Everything is possible for him who believes.' Immediately the boy's father exclaimed, 'I do believe; help me overcome my unbelief!'"

NJB: "...'Everything is possible for one who has faith.' At once the father of the boy cried out, 'I have faith. Help my lack of faith!'"

NEB: "...'Everything is possible to one who has faith.' 'I have faith,' cried the boy's father; 'help me where faith falls short.'"

GNB: "'Everything is possible for the person who has faith.' The father at once cried out, 'I do have faith, but not enough. Help me have more!'"

Two Un-Bibles

The Living Bible is one of the best-selling religious books of our time. It sold 22 million copies in its first seven years in print, in the 1970s, and continues to be very popular, especially in youth programs and college evangelism. Though the book has done immense good in arousing faith and awakening people to the beauty of biblical revelation, it needs to be handled with caution. *The Living Bible* is a paraphrase of the Bible written by Kenneth N. Taylor for his children over a seventeen-year period as he rode a Chicago commuter-train. His style is vivid and exciting. But what makes his translation different from a dynamic equivalence production is his imposition of a particular theological understanding on the text. "The theological lodestar in this book," Taylor writes in the *Preface,* "has been a rigid evangelical position." This approach has caused him to change the text at times, and even to add to it. *The Living Bible* is good spiritual reading, but it is not the Bible.

The Living Bible is more familiar to many in the illustrated edition entitled *The Way,* which was developed by the editors of *Campus Life* magazine. It contains modern photographs, meditations, and introductions on the makeup and use of the book.

A radical departure from customary biblical publishing is *The Reader's Digest Bible* (1982). Advertising itself as a supplement, "not in any way intended to replace the full Biblical text," this book is a condensation of the RSV version of the Bible (minus the deuterocanonicals), reducing its length by 40 percent: the Old Testament by half, the New Testament by a fourth. The editors, headed by biblical expert Dr. Bruce M. Metzger of Princeton University, applied the method long used for

Reader's Digest condensed books in order to make the Bible less formidable for new readers.

The preface distinguishes a condensation from an abridgement. An abridgement reduces the length of a document by eliminating whole sections or by bringing selected passages together; a condensation deals with individual words and lines as well as larger units, to smooth out repetitions. The editors claim they have produced "a text significantly shortened and clarified, yet which retains all sixty-six books, carefully preserves every incident, personality, and teaching of substance, and keeps as well the true essence and flavor of the language." The fact remains that, well done or not, a condensation of the Bible is not the Bible, and cannot replace it.

Part II

Background to the Bible

FIVE

A History of Biblical Times

The God of the Bible is intimately involved in human history. His revelation to the world is not simply a series of declarations or decrees brought on by visions or voices or writings. The biblical message is enmeshed with history and geography, with war and peace, with the lives of individuals and groups of people. The coming of Jesus, called by theology the Incarnation ("en-fleshing"), is the culmination and focus of this process of revelation—God intervening in human history in the ultimate way.

Biblical history is not, therefore, incidental to Bible interpretation. It is more a matrix than a backdrop to revelation. God's word to his people was and is conditioned to their times and situations, their immediate needs, and their abilities to understand. Understanding the historical context of biblical revelation is part of "going back wholly in spirit to those remote centuries of the East" (Pope Pius XII) in order to interpret God's word faithfully.

Pre-History

The biblical lands are part of one of the earliest inhabited regions of the world. Neanderthal skeletons 40,000 years old have been discovered in Palestine, as well as flints from the much earlier Old Stone Age. A few structures, such as a tower in the ruins of Jericho, date to the New Stone Age (7000-4000 B.C.). The immediate predecessors of the Israelites were the Canaanites, a Semitic people who inhabited Palestine from about 3000 B.C. and continued to be influential in the country after the arrival of the Hebrews. The Canaanites were pushed around at various times by the Amorites, Semites from the Syrian area to the north, and by non-Semitic invaders like the Hurrians (called Horites or Hivites in the Bible) from further northwest and northeast. In the narrative of the Exodus, Palestine is referred to as "the country of the Canaanites, Hittites, Amorites, Perizzites, Hivites, and Jebusites" (Ex 3:8), an indication of the variety of tribes and influences in the territory.

The biblical setting is larger than Palestine, however. The geographical canvas for the saga of revelation is known as the Fertile Crescent, a narrow arc of land stretching from the Persian Gulf to Egypt. The water resources in this crescent make life possible around the edge of a vast desert area. Excavations at Tel-Mardikh in northern Syria have revealed the location of ancient Ebla, a commercial center which did business from one end of the Fertile Crescent to the other between 2400 and 2250 B.C. (The finds at Ebla are described in chapter 8.) Some of the earliest evidences of writing come from Mesopotamia, between the Tigris and Euphrates Rivers (in modern Iraq), where the Sumerians developed the cuneiform method of writing around 3000 B.C. It was in this cradle of civilization that biblical history began.

The Patriarchal Period

Abraham lived in the early part of the second millenium B.C. According to the Genesis account (Gn 11:27-32), his family originated in "Ur of the Chaldees," a city in the southern Euphrates valley. From there they migrated north to Haran, which biblical tradition treats as Abraham's homeland. The call of Abraham is usually dated to around 1800 B.C. (Gn 12:1-3). He moved with his wife, Sarah, and his nephew, Lot, to Canaan, where he received a divine promise, then continued on south through the Negeb and into Egypt, and finally returned to settle near Hebron. He is presented as a seminomad in the central hill country of Palestine.

Little is known about Isaac except his birth as the son of the promise and his marriage to Rebekah. Most of the stories about him are either duplicates of Abraham stories or related to his father's life. The story of Isaac's son, Jacob, is more colorful. Forced to flee Canaan because of stealing the blessing of the firstborn from his brother Esau, Jacob returned to the family estates at Haran, where he lived with his uncle Laban and married Leah and Rachel. The interactions of Jacob and Laban make very entertaining reading (Gn 29-31). Jacob left Haran, resolved his quarrel with Esau, and returned to Canaan. His old age is the story of the loss and recovery of his favorite son, Joseph, and the events which took the family to Egypt, where the Hebrews would live for about 400 years until the Exodus.

Moses and the Exodus

The closing chapters of Genesis describe Joseph's rise in the Egyptian court and indicate a continuing period of royal favor for the Hebrew people. Historians associate this turn of events with the period of Hyksos rulers in Egypt. The Hyksos were an Asiatic people who invaded Egypt around 1700 B.C. They were Semitic, which helps explain the favorable treatment accorded Joseph and the family of Jacob. After about 150 years of domination, the Hyksos were cast out by native Egyptians, and the time of Hebrew oppression began: "Then a new king, who knew nothing of Joseph, came to power in Egypt" (Ex 1:8).

The Pharaohs Seti I (1317-1290) and Ramses II (1290-1234) directed vast building programs in connection with the move of the royal residence from Thebes to the northeastern delta location at Tanis. This was probably the setting for the Hebrew slavery described in the Book of Exodus. Moses received his call while in exile among the Midianites at Sinai, then returned and led the Hebrew people across the "Sea of Reeds," a marshy area in the area of the Bitter Lakes between the Mediterranean Sea and the Gulf of Suez. The date of the Exodus is set in the thirteenth century B.C., most commonly during the reign of Ramses II, but by some during the reign of his successor, Merneptah (1234-1220). The Hebrew people looked upon the Exodus as an act of divine redemption and the formative event of their history.

Moses led the people through the desert to the Promised Land. The route of the journey is disputed, depending on the location of Mount Sinai (also called Horeb). The traditional view is that the desert wandering followed a southern route into the Sinai peninsula, and that much of the forty-year period was centered in Kadesh-Barnea in the northeast corner of the Sinai region near the Negeb. The Book of Deuteronomy describes the arrival of the people at Mount Nebo overlooking Canaan, the death of Moses, and the appointment of his successor, Joshua (Dt 34).

Joshua

The Book of Joshua describes the conquest of the Promised Land in epic, even liturgical pageantry. The heroic military campaigns probably did not happen as simply as described. There is archeological evidence for the violent overthrow of some cities around or before 1200 B.C. (Hazor, Bethel, Lachish), but there were also probably minor indecisive skirmishes and a period of gradual assimilation as the Hebrews moved into the land. The Canaanites were not completely displaced. Their presence influenced Israelite history into the time of the divided monarchy. The tribal assembly at Shechem (Jos 24) was probably a covenant-making event of great importance in the creation of a unified people.

Judges

The period of the judges in Israel was approximately 1200-1050 B.C. The judges were local rulers, primarily charismatic military leaders. The scattered Israelite tribes were vulnerable to attack from all sides: from the Philistines on the southwestern coast, from the Moabites and Edomites to the east, and elsewhere from Midianites and Amalekites, and the Canaanites themselves. Lack of national unity kept the Hebrews from establishing their security in the land. It was this problem which eventually prompted the call for a king to bring them together. Samuel, the last judge and the first great prophet, served as the bridge to a new age in Israel.

Saul (1020-1000 B.C.)

The growing Philistine threat finally convinced the scattered tribes to unite against a common enemy. Samuel anointed Saul from the tribe of Benjamin as the first king (1 Sm 10:1). Saul was more successful as a military leader than as a governor, and even his military expertise faded under the pressure of his mental or emotional problems. He had a modest citadel at Gibeah, a few miles northwest of Jerusalem, and probably did not control all the tribes. The Bible presents him as a tragic character, a king paranoid because of the growing power of David and rejected by the prophet who had anointed him. He did, however, create a nation stable enough to endure in the midst of hostile surroundings; this provided a basis for the national developments to come.

David (1000-962 B.C.)

King David was a larger-than-life figure in Israelite tradition. He became a model for the future Messiah. His empire was the center of imaginative longings for generations. David came from Bethlehem in the tribe of Judah. Stories of his youth during the time of Saul present him as a musician and a precocious hero (1 Sm 16-17). David married Saul's daughter, Michal, and became a bosom friend of Saul's son, Jonathan. Saul's fear and jealousy forced David into exile among the Philistines. After the death of Saul and Jonathan at Gilboa, David moved quickly to become the king of Judah at Hebron (2 Sm 1-2). Meanwhile, Saul's kingdom in the north continued under his son Ishbaal (Ishbosheth) from a center at Mahanaim in Transjordan. The strength behind Ishbaal was Abner, the general of Saul's army, who seems to have had designs of his own on the throne. Challenged by Ishbaal, Abner transferred his allegiance to David and helped him take over Saul's kingdom. Shortly thereafter, Abner was murdered by David's general, Joab, in revenge for the death of Joab's younger brother, and probably also to eradicate a rival for the military leadership.

The elders of Saul's northern kingdom of Israel came to Hebron to accept David as their ruler. The Philistines saw their former accomplice as an enemy of dangerous proportions now and attacked in force. David dealt them a decisive defeat (2 Sm 5:17-25). He consolidated his position as king of north and south by capturing Jerusalem, a Jebusite stronghold (2 Sm 5:6-12). The city was naturally well-suited for defense and lay neither in Saul's territory of Benjamin nor in David's territory of Judah. At its greatest extent, David's kingdom stretched from the Lebanon range in the north to deep in the Sinai desert to the south, and from the Mediterranean in the west to the desert in the east.

David's military expertise makes a vivid contrast with his weak hand in personal and family relations. A lengthy narrative (2 Sm 9-20; 1 Kgs 1-2) presents the shadow side of his rule with remarkable honesty. We are able to recognize in the intrigue over the succession the beginnings of problems that would heighten during Solomon's reign and lead to the split of the kingdom.

Solomon (961-922 B.C.)

Solomon, the son of David and Bathsheba, was chosen over several older brothers to be his father's successor. He acted ruthlessly to remove all opposition to his authority (1 Kgs 2:12-46). Solomon preserved and consolidated David's kingdom during a long and relatively peaceful reign. He established treaties with surrounding nations, sealing several of them by marriage to daughters of the foreign rulers. He developed an immense commercial enterprise: sea trade through the Gulf of Aqaba, caravan trade with Arabia, a copper industry, and trade in horses and chariots. He used the chariot as a military weapon for the first time in Israel. Solomon became known as the father of Hebrew wisdom, probably because of the development of historical writing, psalmody, and music during his reign. He inaugurated building on a grand scale, and was especially remembered in later generations as the builder of the Temple.

In the midst of Solomon's prosperity seeds were being planted for a bitter harvest. Solomon's foreign wives brought with them the pagan religions of their homes, and the king did little or nothing to prevent their influence on Israelite worship. Along with the building of the Temple went the construction of an opulent palace and the development of a large bureaucracy. Solomon's commercial ventures were not enough to fund all these projects, so he imposed heavy taxes and drafted Israelites into forced labor. For better management, and also to break down tribal allegiances in favor of united allegiance to the king, he divided the country into twelve administrative districts across tribal lines (1 Kgs 4). These measures produced seething resentment, especially in the north, which felt it was bearing the major burden in supporting the extravagance of the court in the south. Though the kingdom remained intact at Solomon's death, the edifice was beginning to shake and would soon crack apart.

The Divided Monarchy (922-721 B.C.)

Rehoboam (922-915 B.C.) succeeded his father as king in Judah at the death of Solomon in 922 B.C. He then went to Shechem to receive the allegiance of the northern tribes. Unable to detect the fragility of the alliance, Rehoboam refused the northern leaders' demand for an easing of taxation and forced labor (1 Kgs 12:1-25). He rather provoked them into revolt under Jeroboam I (922-901 B.C.), and from this moment the kingdom of David was divided into the northern kingdom of ten tribes (Israel), which would last until its fall to the Assyrians in 721 B.C., and the smaller southern kingdom of Judah, which would be destroyed by the Babylonians in 587 B.C.

Jeroboam took measures to divert the attraction of the Jerusalem Temple as the focus of Hebrew faith. He established northern sanctuaries at the ancient religious centers of Dan and Bethel. The later Deuteronomist editors of 1 and 2 Kings looked on this worship at other sanctuaries as "the sin of Jeroboam," a major cause of the downfall of Israel. The powerful monarchy had been replaced by two weak states in Israel and Judah. The Egyptian ruler Shishak took advantage of this weakness to reestablish Egyptian influence in Palestine. His attacks in

918 B.C. left both North and South reeling. All thought of a forced reunification of the kingdom by either side ended during the Egyptian assault.

Rehoboam was succeeded in Judah by his son, Abijah, who ruled for only two years (915-913 B.C.). He temporarily took back part of the northern land, including the sanctuary at Bethel, but the line was difficult to hold. His son, Asa (913-873 B.C.), was faced with Egyptian invasion from the south; and though he managed to defeat this enemy, his attention was distracted long enough for Israel's king, Baasha (900-877 B.C.), to send armies into Ramah, five miles north of Jerusalem. Asa called on his ally to the north, Ben-hadad I of Damascus, with whose help he managed to secure the capital again (1 Kgs 15:16-22).

Jeroboam had established his capital at Shechem, but later moved to Tirzah a few miles to the north; later the capital was located in Samaria. The northern dynasty was even more unstable than the capital's location. Judah had the tradition of the Davidic line, but in Israel kingship was more charismatic. Ideally, Israel's kings were designated by divine decree through the prophets; but assassination was often the reality behind the accession of a king. Jeroboam's son, Nadab (901-900 B.C.) was killed by Baasha, whose son, Elah (877-876 B.C.), was killed by Zimri (876 B.C.). Zimri ruled a week before taking his own life at the advance of Omri's army.

The House of Omri

Though given little attention in the Bible (1 Kgs 16:23-28), Omri (876-869 B.C.) was one of the strongest kings of Israel. Assyrian records referred to Israel for generations as the "house of Omri." He firmly established the northern kingdom and consolidated his own family on the throne. In sealing a pact with Tyre, though, he committed the costly mistake of marrying his son Ahab (869-850 B.C.) to the Tyrian princess, Jezebel, who marshalled all her efforts to promoting the worship of Baal in Israel. It was at this time that the prophet Elijah arose to defend the pure Yahwistic faith. The people ultimately rejected the paganizing influence of the Omri family. At the prompting of the prophet Elisha, Jehu, the general of the army, overthrew the last of the Omrides, Jehoram (849-842 B.C.), and became the first king (842-815 B.C.) of a new dynasty.

Meanwhile, greater stability was maintained in Judah, where the Davidic succession remained secure and where there was less pagan religious influence. Jehoshaphat (873-849 B.C.) was an able king who instituted a series of judicial reforms and established a court of appeals in Jerusalem. He entered into an alliance with Israel during the reign of Ahab. His successors, Jehoram (849-842 B.C.; his name and his period of rule were identical to that of his counterpart in the north) and Ahaziah (842 B.C.), were weak kings. Ahaziah had the bad luck to be visiting in Israel during the purge of Jehu and was slain. His mother, Athaliah (842-837 B.C.), who had been the power behind the throne, then seized the scepter and reinforced the cult of Baal which she had already introduced in Jerusalem. But growing public resentment eventually brought her assassination by the high priest, Jehoiada, and the Temple guards (2 Kgs 11:4-16), and her replacement on the throne by the seven-year-old son of Ahaziah, Jehoash (837-800 B.C.). This king ruled adequately as long as Jehoiada lived to guide him. But after the high priest's death, Jehoash fell into religious laxity and was assassinated himself by some of his officials (2 Kgs 12:21).

At this time the northern kingdom experienced a resurgence under Jehoash of Israel (801-786 B.C.) and Jeroboam II (786-746 B.C.). Jehoash was more enterprising than his namesake in the south. He recaptured much of the land lost by his father, Jehoahaz (815-801 B.C.), and established Israel's superiority over Judah. This was largely because of the ineptitude of Amaziah of Judah (800-783 B.C.), who provoked an assault which Jehoash did not want to make (2 Kgs 14:8-14). Amaziah's failures led to his assassination and replacement by Uzziah (or Azariah: 783-742 B.C.). With Uzziah on the throne in the south and Jeroboam II ruling in the north, the two sister states achieved their greatest prosperity since the division of the monarchy.

In Israel, however, Amos and Hosea spoke out against the hidden corruption in Jeroboam II's kingdom. After his death, political instability took over again, with four of the six succeeding rulers falling to assassins. This coincided with the expansion of Assyria under Tiglath-pileser III (745-728 B.C.). Pekah (king of Israel from 737-732 B.C.) invaded Judah in 734 B.C. to try to force the southern kingdom under Ahaz (735-715 B.C.) to join a coalition of defense with Damascus against Assyria. Instead, Ahaz sent tribute to Tiglath-pileser, asking for help against Israel. The Assyrians destroyed the coalition and conquered Galilee. Pekah's successor, Hoshea (732-724 B.C.), maintained Israel as a vassal of Assyria until 726 B.C., when he rashly assumed that the accession of a new Assyrian king, Shalmaneser V (726-722 B.C.), was the moment to seek help from Egypt against the overlords. Assyria invaded and took Hoshea prisoner. After a long siege under Sargon II (721-705 B.C.), the Assyrians captured the city of Samaria and deported its inhabitants to Upper Mesopotamia (2 Kgs 17:1-6). The kingdom of Israel came to an end in 721 B.C.

The Last Days of Judah (721-587 B.C.)

Ahaz's decision to become the vassal of Assyria saved Judah from the same fate as Israel, but resulted in other serious consequences. Political subservience demanded recognition of the overlord's god in addition to the local deity. Ahaz was not very religious anyway, and acquiesced readily in setting up an altar to the Mesopotamian god Hadad-Rimmon in the Jerusalem Temple (2 Kgs 16:10-18). Ahaz even sacrificed his own son in the fire rites of the Canaanite god Moloch (16:3). His reign was remembered as one of the worst periods of apostasy in history.

Ahaz's son, Hezekiah (715-687 B.C.), began immediately, but slowly, to reverse the apostasy and the subservience to Assyria. The prophets Isaiah and Micah had already been active in denouncing the policies of Ahaz. Isaiah worked very closely with Hezekiah. The king instituted a religious reform. He strengthened the defenses of Jerusalem; one of his most striking achievements in this regard was the chiseling of a 1,749-foot tunnel to bring water from the spring Gihon into the city. When Sargon II died in 705 B.C., his successor Sennacherib (705-681 B.C.) was greeted with widespread revolt in the extended Assyrian empire. Sennacherib responded quickly and effectively. Hezekiah sympathized with the revolt, but hesitated to involve Israel. The Assyrians attacked him anyway, coming to the gates of Jerusalem in 701 B.C. Isaiah urged Hezekiah to trust in Yahweh and promised deliverance. This came through a pestilence among the Assyrians which was seen as divine intervention (2 Kgs 19).

Hezekiah's son, Manasseh (687-642 B.C.), returned to the policies of his grandfather, Ahaz. His reign is notorious for a policy of subservience to Assyria in religious matters, for widespread oppression, and for murder. His son, Amon (642-640 B.C.), continued in the same vein, and was assassinated after a short reign.

Josiah (640-609 B.C.) was only eight years old when he succeeded his father. By the time he was old enough to rule, the Assyrian empire was crumbling before the onslaughts of Babylon. In 621 B.C., a copy of the Book of Deuteronomy, which had been forbidden reading during the reigns of Manasseh and Amon, was discovered in the Temple. Josiah based a full-scale religious reform on this book of the Law, repudiating Assyrian gods and centralizing the Yahwistic worship in Jerusalem (2 Kgs 22-23). He proclaimed independence from Assyria and proceeded to reclaim territories to the north that had been taken from David's kingdom. After the fall of Nineveh, the Assyrian capital (612 B.C.), Josiah continued to work against all attempts to restore the power of Assyria. It was in pursuit of this goal that Josiah was killed by the Egyptians at Megiddo. Next to David, Josiah was the king held highest in the hearts of the Israelites. His contemporary, Jeremiah, spoke of him as a man who "did what was right and just ... dispensed justice to the weak and the poor" (Jer 22:15-16).

Josiah's reform was reversed under his son, Jehoiakim (609-598 B.C.), who was established on the throne in place of his brother, Jehoahaz, by the Egyptians. After the Egyptians were defeated by the Babylonians (605 B.C.), Jehoiakim submitted to the Babylonian king, Nebuchadnezzar II (604-562 B.C.), but later rebelled, calling down the wrath of Nebuchadnezzar and the capture of Jerusalem in 597 B.C. Jehoiakim died three months before the fall of the city and was succeeded by his son Jehoiachin (Jeconiah), who reigned only three months before being deposed and deported to Babylon. With him went most of the leaders and craftsmen of Jerusalem (2 Kgs 24:10-17). He was replaced by his uncle, Zedekiah (597-587 B.C.) who, though he was a son of Josiah, was considered a usurper by Israelite believers. They saw in Jehoiachin the true heir of David and hoped that he would eventually return from exile to restore his reign.

Zedekiah was weak and vacillating. Against Jeremiah's advice, he revolted against Babylon in 589 B.C. Nebuchadnezzar was less patient this time than in 597 B.C. He destroyed the city completely, razing the Temple of Solomon, and took another large group of Israelites into exile in Babylon, leaving only "some of the country's poor" (2 Kgs 25:12).

The Babylonian Exile

Nebuchadnezzar installed Gedaliah, a Jerusalemite, as governor of the ruined city. The spirit of rebellion persisted, and Gedaliah was assassinated by a member of the royal Jewish line. Fearing reprisals from Babylon, a large number of the remaining Israelites fled to Egypt. Meanwhile, the exiles in Babylon were given relatively free movement and began to adjust to the new conditions.

The tenacious Israelite faith kept alive Hebrew hopes and Hebrew identity. During these years, the exiles built up their religious traditions, collecting and editing the narratives and law codes, writing down old psalms and composing new ones, and in general establishing the firm basis for a future Jewish life. Prophets like Ezekiel and Second Isaiah (Is 40-55) encouraged the faithful Israelites. Though some of the people adapted too well to life in Babylon and gave up hope of a return to Israel, a hard core kept the hope intact.

Babylon remained powerful during the long reign of Nebuchadnezzar, but decline began after his death in 562 B.C. The throne changed hands three times in seven years before Nabonidus (555-538 B.C.) established a longer reign. But the empire continued its decline. For eight years Nabonidus transferred his residence to the Arabian desert, leaving the government in the hands of his son Belshazzar. Meanwhile, a new power in world affairs was emerging. Cyrus II of Persia (559-529 B.C.) at first enlisted the help of Nabonidus in taking control of Media, then turned on Babylon. Around 550 B.C. he became the hope of the exiled Israelites (Is 44:28), and in 539 B.C. he conquered Babylon.

Within a year of his conquest, Cyrus issued a decree for the restoration of Jewish life and worship in Palestine (Ezr 1:2-4). His policy allowed subject peoples their own cultural identity within the framework of the larger empire. The Israelites planned for the return to Jerusalem under Sheshbazzar, a member of the Jewish royal family (Ezr 1:8). Some of the people, of course, would never return. Thus began the feature of Judaism known as the Diaspora, or dispersion. Jews remaining in Babylon and Egypt at this time kept their faith alive in the synagogues and supported developments in Jerusalem by prayers and donations.

The Return to Israel

The biblical accounts emphasize the disappointment and disillusionment which faced the exuberant exiles on their return to Jerusalem. The city was in ruins, the sparse population wretched. Worship had declined in purity. Surrounding neighbors were hostile. Sheshbazzar faded from the scene to be replaced by the governor Zerubbabel, a descendant of David. His counterpart as religious leader was the high priest, Joshua. These two laid initial plans for the reconstruction of the Temple, but in refusing to accept the help of residents of the land, they stirred up the ill feeling which led to hostilities between Jews and Samaritans (Ezr 4).

Enthusiasm for the new Temple subsided in the face of the immense work of carving out an existence in the ruined land. When, after nearly twenty years, the Temple still lay in ruins, the prophets Haggai and Zechariah challenged the Jews to follow through with their building plans (Hg 2:1-4). The new Temple was finished in 515 B.C.

Nehemiah and Ezra (445-395 B.C.)

The restoration of the Temple did not bring with it a golden age. The prophecy of Malachi tells of priestly corruption fifty years later. In 445 B.C., the bad news reaching Persia stirred Nehemiah, the cupbearer to the king, into action (Neh 1:1-3). With royal support, he headed a mission to Jerusalem and succeeded in having the walls of the city rebuilt in fifty-two days despite the violent opposition of the Samaritans and other hostile neighbors. Because the city was badly underpopulated, Nehemiah persuaded the Jews to cast lots so that one in ten would move into Jerusalem.

Nehemiah remained as governor in Judah until 433 B.C., achieving important reforms in worship and social justice. He returned to the Persian court, satisfied that Jerusalem had been saved. But when he returned a couple of years later, Nehemiah found new abuses in Jerusalem (Neh 13:6-11). He again implemented vigorous reforms regularizing the work and payment of the Levites, supervising Sabbath observance, and establishing strict rules against the intermarriage of Jews with foreigners.

Nehemiah's mission was followed by that of the priest-scribe Ezra, also sent with the approval and support of the Persian ruler (Ezr 7:1-10). Ezra took even stronger measures against intermarriage. He demanded that those involved in mixed marriages separate. Then he organized a formal ratification of the covenant of Moses after the Feast of Tabernacles (Neh 10:1-27). Later tradition considered Ezra a second Moses and attributed the definitive editing of the Books of the Law to him.

We know very little of Jewish history during the final century of Persian rule after the reforms of Nehemiah and Ezra. The biblical books of Obadiah, Joel, and Jonah, produced around 400 B.C., indicate that a certain arrogance accompanied the reforms. The work of "the Chronicler" (the writer or writers responsible for the books of Ezra, Nehemiah, and Chronicles), also dated to this era, is defensive and triumphalistic. The Samaritans found themselves hopelessly excluded from Jewish life and worship; they built their own temple on Mount Gerizim in the latter part of the fourth century.

Judah was relatively self-enclosed and isolated from the rest of the world during these years. But the Jews were still part of the Persian empire and affected by its policies. It was during this time that Hebrew began to be displaced by Aramaic, a widely diffused Semitic language normative in the empire, as the language of everyday discourse. The high priests gave in reluctantly to this inevitable development, preserving Hebrew as the language of worship and study.

Alexander and the Greek Empire (333-175 B.C.)

In 336 B.C., Alexander the Great succeeded to the throne in Macedonia. After imposing unity on Greece, he turned toward the east. At the decisive battle of Issus (present-day southern Turkey near Syria) in 333 B.C. he defeated the Persian army and began the period of Greek domination in western Asia. He turned southward from Syria and proceeded along the Mediterranean coast of Palestine until he reached Egypt. He was welcomed as the new pharaoh and established the city of Alexandria in 332 B.C. Judah came under Alexander's control at this time and felt the brunt of his strong hellenizing program.

Ten years after the establishment of his Greek empire, Alexander died at the age of thirty-three. His kingdom fell to pieces among his warring generals. Ptolemy seized control of Egypt, while Seleucus became ascendant over Babylon and regions west all the way to Syria. At first, Ptolemy and his family, who were relatively benevolent overlords, controlled Palestine. But in 198 B.C., the Seleucid ruler Antiochus III defeated Ptolemy V at Panion, north of the Sea of Galilee, and Palestine came under Syrian rule.

Antiochus III accorded the Jews the same privileges they had enjoyed under the Persians. But in 190 B.C., trying to expand his kingdom toward the west, he received a crushing defeat at the hands of the Romans. Three years later, he was assassinated and his son, Seleucus IV (187-175 B.C.) took over. Under this king, subjects began to feel the tax burdens of a declining kingdom. Seleucus even tried to take funds from the Jerusalem Temple. Seleucus was killed by his chancellor and succeeded by his brother, Antiochus IV Epiphanes (175-163 B.C.), who had been held hostage in Rome since the defeat of his father.

The Maccabean Revolt

In an effort to unify his empire for defense, Antiochus IV fostered universal Hellenism, including worship of Zeus and the other Greek gods (1 Mc 1:41-43). This policy put him on a collision course with Judaism. He appointed a high priest supportive of his policies and eventually forbade circumcision and other Jewish observances, using Temple funds for his own projects. The crowning blow was the introduction of the cult of Olympian Zeus into the Temple (2 Mc 6:2) and the erection of an altar of the pagan deity there. This was the "horrible abomination" referred to in the Book of Daniel (9:27) written during these years. Rebellion finally erupted in 167 B.C. when Mattathias, head of a staunch Jewish family, refused to offer pagan sacrifice and rallied a revolutionary band to the Judean hills.

When Mattathias died in 166 B.C., the leadership passed to his son Judas Maccabeus ("the hammer"), who led a full-scale war against the forces of Antiochus. He won an impressive series of battles culminating in the defeat of Antiochus' regent, Lysias, and the purification of the Temple of Jerusalem in 164 B.C., an event that is still celebrated by the annual Jewish feast of Hannukah (1 Mc 4:36-59). Judas continued his campaign for complete Jewish independence until he fell in battle in 160 B.C.

Judas was succeeded by his younger brother, Jonathan (160-143 B.C.), who maintained his autonomy by playing the claimants to the Seleucid throne against one another. He accepted the high priesthood from one of the Seleucid overlords, Alexander Balas (150-145 B.C.). After his death, Jonathan was followed by an older brother, Simon (143-134 B.C.), who managed to get an official decree of independence from

Demetrius II, in 142 B.C. (1 Mc 13:41). Though the Maccabees were not of the Zadokite, or high-priestly, line, officials and people decreed that Simon would be accepted as their true ruler and high priest "until a true prophet arises" (1 Mc 14:41). This angered some of the Jewish purists, and the beginning of the separatist Essene movement may date from this time. It is possible that the Wicked Priest mentioned in the Dead Sea Scrolls from Qumran is Simon. Simon established a period of peaceful rule until his assassination by a son-in-law in 134 B.C. He was succeeded by his son, John Hyrcanus (134-104 B.C.). The rulers of this line were named Hasmoneans after an ancestor of Mattathias.

John held his kingdom precariously until 128 B.C. when Antiochus VII was slain in battle. Then he began to expand the horizons of Judea, reaching across the Jordan and subduing the hostile territory of Edom, where he forced the inhabitants to accept circumcision and the Mosaic law. He went north to Samaria and destroyed the Samaritan temple on Mount Gerizim. During his reign the two groups of Pharisees and Sadducees emerged. The Pharisees, alarmed at the secular character of John's administration, broke with the Hasmoneans.

Subsequent events bore witness to the moral deterioration of Judaism with the Hasmoneans as ruling high priests. John Hyrcanus bequeathed the rule to his wife, but at his death she was imprisoned by their son, Aristobulus I, who then took over the throne (104-103 B.C.). He imprisoned three of his brothers and murdered a fourth. Poetic justice seemed to follow when his widow, Salome Alexandra, freed the brothers and married one of them, the new ruler Alexander Janneus (103-76). Alexander extended the boundaries of Israel almost to the limits of David's kingdom. When a group of Jews turned against him unsuccessfully, Alexander had eight hundred of them, along with their wives and children, executed—a dinner entertainment while he feasted with his concubines.

Salome (76-67 B.C.) took over the rule after the death of Alexander, but appointed her elder son Hyrcanus II high priest. After her death, Hyrcanus II and his younger brother Aristobulus II fought over the kingship. Aristobulus became king and high priest but Hyrcanus continued to plot his downfall. Their wrangling brought about the intervention of Rome in 63 B.C. The Roman general Pompey marched on Jerusalem, imprisoned Aristobulus, and appointed Hyrcanus high priest. By this act the independence won by the Maccabees came to an end.

Roman Rule in Palestine

Pompey made Palestine part of the Roman province of Syria, whose major cities were Antioch and Damascus. Rome ruled through a governor, Scaurus, but left religious authority in the hands of the high priest, who was influenced by Antipater of Idumaea (south of Palestine), father of Herod the Great. Hyrcanus II and Antipater played their cards cagily during the quarrel between Pompey and Julius Caesar (49-48 B.C.), supporting Pompey at first, then switching to Caesar's side when his victory seemed likely. When the triumphant Caesar visited Syria in 47 B.C. Hyrcanus was given rule as ethnarch (ruler of a people) in addition to his high priesthood, and Antipater was made prefect or procurator of Judea.

Antipater had his sons Phasael and Herod named governors of Judea and Galilee. But when Caesar was assassinated in 44

B.C. and Antipater one year later, the future of Antipater's family darkened. Herod remained in the favor of Roman rivals Cassius and Mark Antony during the tumult following Caesar's death. When Parthians from the Persian area took advantage of chaos in the Syrian province to invade Palestine in 40 B.C., Antigonus, the nephew of the high priest, sided with the Parthians and was named high priest and king. He caused Phasael to commit suicide and had Hyrcanus' ears cut off so he could no longer be a rival for the high priesthood; Herod barely escaped with his life. Supported by Antony and Octavian, Herod was named by the Romans king of Judea (and later Samaria). He returned to Palestine and fought for three years before wresting his kingdom away from Antigonus, whom Herod crucified and beheaded in 37 B.C.

Herod's reign (37-4 B.C.) is noted for vicious acts of brutality within and outside his family, and for major building achievements. He built not only theaters, palaces, and fortresses, but even new cities. He supported Roman emperor worship, which added to the resentment Jews already felt toward him. To curry favor with his subjects he began the restoration of the Second Temple (built in 515 B.C.) in 20 B.C. This work was continued during the whole lifetime of Jesus and was not finished until A.D. 63, seven years before the Temple was destroyed.

In the Days of Jesus (4 B.C.-A.D. 29)

The dating of the birth of Jesus to A.D. 1 is due to a miscalculation in the sixth century A.D. Jesus was born during the last days of Herod, while Augustus was emperor (Lk 2:1). Augustus (27 B.C.- A.D. 14) was the Octavian who vied successfully with Mark Antony for Roman rule after the death of Julius Caesar.

He received his new title (Augustus means *majestic*) as a mark of gratitude from the Senate for the establishment of peace in the empire. At the time of Jesus' birth, Roman supervision of Palestine was exercised by a legate for the province of Syria.

After Herod's death, dissension over his successor broke out immediately. The Jews were hoping to be rid of the Herod family. Various "messiahs" put themselves forward, fostering uprisings in different parts of the country. The Romans sent in a temporary procurator, Varus, who quelled the riots and sent a clear message to all rebels by crucifying two thousand Jews throughout the land. Herod's sons hurried to the Roman court and obtained the following distribution of power from Augustus: Archelaus received the title ethnarch and half the kingdom including Judea and Samaria; Antipas and Philip were named tetrarchs (rulers of fourths of the kingdom), Antipas of Galilee and southern Transjordan, Philip of northern Transjordan.

By the time Jesus began his public ministry (A.D. 27), some adjustments had taken place. Augustus had been replaced by the emperor Tiberius (A.D. 14-37). Antipas (the Herod of the Gospel stories: Lk 3:1; 23:6-12) ruled his territory until A.D. 39, when the emperor Gaius Caligula banished him to Gaul for being power-hungry. Philip died in office in A.D. 34. Archelaus was unable to play the sensitive role demanded at his post in Jerusalem. He antagonized the Jews with his highhanded ways and by imitating his father's harshness and cruelty (see Mt 2:22). In A.D. 6, a delegation of leading citizens from Judea and Samaria went to Rome to lodge a formal complaint against Archelaus. He was deposed and banished to Gaul, where he died about ten years later. Augustus decided to govern the troublesome region directly through a Roman procurator. The first of these was Coponius (A.D. 6-9); during the time of Jesus' ministry the procurator was Pontius Pilate (A.D. 26-36). It was during Pilate's rule that the events of the gospel story took place, from John the Baptist's preaching ministry to the death and resurrection of Jesus.

Before the Jewish Revolt (A.D. 30-66)

Pontius Pilate was no wiser than Archelaus in his administration of Judea and Samaria. The last straw in a series of offenses came in A.D. 35 when he attacked a group of Samaritans on pilgrimage to Mount Gerizim, killing some and imprisoning the rest. He was recalled to Rome. In A.D. 37 Tiberius died and was succeeded by Caligula (A.D. 37-41). He appointed Agrippa I, grandson of Herod the Great, ruler of Philip's vacated tetrarchy, and added the tetrarchy of Antipas when the latter was exiled in A.D. 39. Under the emperor Claudius (A.D. 41-54), Agrippa I received also the ethnarchy of Archelaus, thus becoming ruler of a territory similar in size to that of Herod the Great from A.D. 41 to 44. Agrippa I is the "Herod" of Acts 12:2 who beheaded James the brother of John. Agrippa himself died suddenly at the imperial games at Caesarea soon afterward (Acts 12:20-23).

Instead of allowing a king to succeed Agrippa, Claudius returned to the procurator system for administrating Palestine. Agrippa II, the king's son, ruled fringe areas of the country, including part of Galilee, until late in the century. He was the Agrippa asked by the procurator Porcius Festus (A.D. 60-62) to hear Paul's story in Acts 25-26. The Roman procurators ruled the land during this time with general insensitivity to Jewish culture. Antonius Felix (A.D. 52-60), under whom Paul was first imprisoned at Caesarea (Acts 24), was one of the worst. The last of the procurators was Gessius Florus (A.D. 64-66), who aggravated the raw feelings of his subjects by plundering lands and sacking towns while taking bribes from bandits.

The Jewish Revolt and Its Aftermath (A.D. 66-135)

The Zealots, a group of Jewish nationalists, had been organized in A.D. 6 as a reaction to the Roman tax enrollment in Judea and Samaria. Because they centered in Galilee, the name "Galilean" came to have the overtone of "revolutionary." Judas the Galilean, mentioned by Gamaliel (Acts 5:37) was one of the first organizers. When the outrages of Florus stirred the Jews to rebellion in A.D. 66, a descendant of Judas, Menahem, was the principal aide of the leader, Eleazar. Josephus, the future historian, was given charge of Galilee.

The Jews won the first skirmishes until the Emperor Nero (A.D. 54-68) sent the experienced commander, Vespasian, to guide military operations. He subdued Galilee in A.D. 67 and was moving on Jerusalem when Nero died in 68. The fighting halted while Vespasian waited for signals from Rome, where three emperors succeeded Nero within a year. Vespasian himself was proclaimed emperor on July 1, 69; he returned to Rome, leaving his son Titus in command. Meanwhile the Jews were weakened by strife among themselves. The aristocratic patriots in Jerusalem, led by the priests, would not combine with the left-wing Zealots. The Zealot leader John of Gischala and his followers blockaded themselves in the Temple while the Idumaean strongman, Simon bar Giora, ruled in the city. According to the Christian historian Eusebius, the Jerusalem Christians fled to Pella in Transjordan during this time. Titus advanced on Jerusalem in the spring of A.D. 70 and by September had burned the Temple and razed the city walls. The revolt was crushed, though the final group of resisters at Masada was not conquered until A.D. 73.

Palestine lost its procuratorship at this time and became a Roman province. This meant that the Jews no longer had national identity within the empire. The Romans owned the land now, not the Jews, who were homeless and officially name-less. Because the Temple was destroyed, sacrifice and the priest-hood vanished. A group of rabbis under Johanan ben Zakkai formed a school in Jabneh (Jamnia) to build up the religious traditions of the nation as earlier Jewish leaders had done dur-ing the Babylonian Exile. A new age of Jewish-Christian rela-tions began. In order to protect a weak and battered Judaism, the rabbis outlawed all but the purest Pharisaic elements. Christians, many of whom had maintained their Jewish life and worship (Acts 2:46), were now excluded from the synagogue. The bitterness that grew up between the two religious groups at this time is reflected in the Gospels of Matthew and John.

Titus succeeded his father as emperor (A.D. 79-81). Both of them were remarkably tolerant of the Jews and Christians after their campaigns in Palestine. Domitian, brother of Titus, contin-ued this policy during the first part of his long reign (A.D. 81-96). But during his final three or four years, Domitian permitted a more aggressive promotion of the emperor cult, which entailed harassment of Jews and Christians, particularly in Asia Minor.

After a break in the persecution under the aged Emperor Nerva (A.D. 96-98), oppression of Jews and Christians contin-ued during the long reigns of Trajan (A.D. 98-117) and Hadrian (A.D. 117-138). These two rulers, like Domitian, promoted the emperor cult as a test of patriotism. A large-scale persecution of Christians in Asia Minor is reflected in the letters of Pliny the Younger, governor of Bithynia, to Trajan about A.D. 113. Jewish Zealotism erupted in the Diaspora in A.D. 115 while Trajan was occupied with campaigns against the Parthians. The war began in Cyrene and Egypt in northern Africa and spread to Mesopotamia, but was put down in A.D. 117.

Jewish resentment continued to seethe during the reign of Hadrian. In A.D. 132 another war for the liberation of Jerusalem broke out, the Second Jewish Revolt, under Simon ben Kosiba (Bar Cochba). The precipitating causes were Hadrian's general banning of circumcision in the empire and his plan to build a Hellenistic Roman city on the site of Jerusalem. The Jews were able to keep Rome at bay for three years by guerilla warfare, but the rebellion was crushed in A.D. 135. In the early 1950s, letters from Bar Cochba to rebel soldiers in hiding were discovered in the caves of Wadi Murabba`at near the Dead Sea.

Hadrian followed through on his plan to build a Roman city at Jerusalem. He named it Aelia Capitolina (from his family name, Aelius); the Temple area became the site of a sanctuary of Zeus and Hadrian, and Calvary became the site of a temple of Jupiter, Juno, and Venus. He banned Jews from Jerusalem, decreeing (in Eusebius' words) that "the whole Jewish nation should be absolutely prevented from that time on from entering even the district around Jerusalem, so that not even from a distance could it see its ancestral home."

Historical Chart			
Dates	**Events**	**Biblical Figures**	**Composition of Biblical Writings**
1800 B.C. 1700 1600 1500 1400 1300		Abraham Isaac Jacob	
	Exodus from Egypt Covenant at Sinai	Moses	
1200 1100	Invasion of Canaan Rule by Judges	Joshua Gideon Deborah Samson	
	Samuel Saul (1020-1000) David (1000-962) Solomon (961-922)	Jonathan Nathan	*Court History:* 2 Samuel 9-20; 2 Kings 1-2 *Yahwist (J) writing*
	Division of Kingdom 922 **Judah** **Israel** Rehoboam Jeroboam I (922-915) (922-901) Abijah Nadab (915-913) (901-900) Asa Baasha		

900	(913-873) (877-876)
	             Zimri (876)
	             Omri
	             (876-869)
	             Ahab
	             (869-850)
		Elijah	*Elohist (E) writing*

Historical Chart				
Dates	**Events**		**Biblical Figures**	**Composition of Biblical Writings**
800	Jehoram (849-842) Ahaziah (842) Athaliah (842-837) Johoash (837-800) Amaziah (800-783) Uzziah (783-742) Jotham (742-735) Ahaz (735-715)	Ahaziah (850-849) Jehoram (849-842) Jehu (842-815) Joahaz (815-801) Jehoash (801-786) Jeroboam II (786-746) Zechariah (746-745) Shallum (745) Menahem (745-738) Pekaiah (738-737) Pekah (737-732) Hoshea (732-724) Fall of Samaria (721) Exile of Israel	Elisha Jehoiada Amos Hosea Isaiah Micah	 Amos Hosea Isaiah 1-39 Micah

Historical Chart

Dates	Events	Biblical Figures	Composition of Biblical Writings
700	Hezekiah (715-687)		Deuteronomy 12-26
	Manasseh (687-642)		
	Amon (642-640)		
	Josiah (640-609)	Zephaniah Jeremiah Nahum	Zephaniah Jeremiah Nahum
	Jehoahaz (Shallum) (609)		
600	Jehoiakim (Jeconiah) (598-597)		
	Zedekiah (Mattaniah) (597-587)		
	Fall of Jerusalem Destruction of Temple (587)		
	Exile in Babylon (587-538)	Ezekiel Second Isaiah	Lamentations Ezekiel
	Gedaliah (587)		Isaiah 40-55
			Pentateuch: Genesis, Exodus, Leviticus, Numbers, Deuteronomy

Historical Chart

Dates	Events	Biblical Figures	Composition of Biblical Writings
			Edition of Deuteronomic History: Joshua, Judges, 1-2 Samuel, 1-2 Kings Some Psalms
500	Sheshbazzar (538) Zerubbabel (538-510) Second Temple Dedication Nehemiah (445-433, 431-?) Ezra (428-395)	Joshua Haggai Zechariah Malachi	Haggai Zechariah 1-8 *Priestly (P) editing* Malachi Job Proverbs Psalms Song of Songs Ruth Isaiah 56-66
400		Obadiah Joel	Obadiah Joel Jonah *Work of Chronicler:* 1-2 Chronicles, Ezra Nehemiah Zechariah 9-14
	Persian rule replaced by Greek rule Rule by Ptolemies of Egypt (323)		

Historical Chart			
Dates	**Events**	**Biblical Figures**	**Composition of Biblical Writings**
300			Ecclesiastes Esther Tobit
200	Rule by Seleucids of Syria (198)		Sirach Ecclesiasticus
	Persecution Maccabean Revolt (167-164)	Mattathias	Daniel
	Rededication of Temple (164)		
	Judas Maccabeus (166-160)		
	Jonathan (160-143)		
	Simon (143-134)		Judith
	John Hyrcanus (134-104)		2 Maccabees
	Aristobulus (104-103)		
100	Alexander Janneus (103-76)		1 Maccabees
	Salome Alexandra (76-67)		
	Aristobulus II (67-63)		
	Antipater (63-43, procurator)		Baruch
	Hyrcanus II (47-40 ethnarch)		Wisdom
	Antigonus (40-37)		
	Herod the Great (374)		
	Tetrarchs:	Birth of	
A.D. 1	Archelaus (4 B.C.- A.D. 6)	Jesus	
	Antipas (4 B.C.-A.D. 39)	(4 B.C.)	
	Philip (4 B.C.-A.D. 34)		
	Procurators of Judea (6-66)		
	Pontius Pilate (26-36)	Death of Jesus (A.D. 29)	

Historical Chart

Dates	Events	Biblical Figures	Composition of Biblical Writings
	Agrippa I (37-44)		
			1-2 Thessalonians
	Antonius Felix (52-60)		Galatians
			Philippians
			1-2 Corinthians
			Romans
	Porcius Festus (60-62)		Philemon
	Lucceius Albinus (62-64)		Colossians
	Gessius Florus (64-66)		
	The Jewish Revolt (66-70)		Mark
	Fall of Jerusalem (70)		James, Jude
			Ephesians
			Titus, 1 & 2
			Timothy
			Luke, Acts
			Matthew
			Hebrews
			1 Peter
			John
			Revelation
100			1, 2, 3 John
			2 Peter
	Second Jewish Revolt (132-135)		

SIX

The Hebrew Scriptures I:
Law and Prophets

The Christian Scriptures make up only one fourth of the Bible. The bulk of the volume consists of the Jewish writings known as the Hebrew Scriptures (though some parts were written in Aramaic and Greek). Christians more commonly refer to this first part of the Bible as the Old Testament to contrast it with the New Testament of Christianity. This usage comes from the early Christian writings, which refer to the "old" (2 Cor 3:14) or "first" covenant (Heb 9:15) of God with Israel, and the "new" covenant in Jesus Christ (Lk 22:20; 1 Cor 11:25). The word "testament" in the titles of the two parts of the Bible is from the Latin word *testamentum* used to translate the Hebrew and Greek words for "covenant."

Christians believe that the whole Bible proclaims the inspired word of God, but that the meaning of God's revelation is fully comprehended only in Christ. Therefore, the Old Testament is interpreted in light of the New Testament. Revelation is progressive up to the coming of Christ. God did not drop his full message of truth into the world as a neatly packaged product. He gradually coaxed his people along according to their ability to understand and respond, preparing them for the complete and definitive revelation.

That does not mean, however, that the Hebrew Scriptures

are expendable as a preliminary of the past. This was the mistake of Marcion (see chapter 3). The teaching of Jesus and the preaching and writing of the first Christians presuppose the "law of Moses and ... the prophets and psalms" (Lk 24:44). Christianity is the full flowering of the revelation to Israel. Our understanding of the central themes of the Old Testament is essential for interpretation of the New Testament. The description of God's love and care in Isaiah and the Psalms, for example, provides the context for Jesus' revelation of his Father.

Law, Prophets, and Writings

Modern Jews refer to their Bible as *Tanak,* an acronym for Torah (Law), Nevi'im (Prophets), and Ketuvim (Writings), the three major divisions. These sections are roughly chronological, Torah comprising the first five books (Pentateuch) and dealing with creation, Exodus, and covenant; Prophets containing, besides the prophetic oracles, the history of the people from Joshua to the Exile, and Writings containing later productions. This arrangement depends more on the subject than on the time of writing; the creation stories, for example, were written after the Exodus.

Law

The first five books of the Bible were known as the Torah in Hebrew and as the Pentateuch in Greek. They contain God's Law as revealed to Moses but much else besides: creation stories, patriarchal narratives, the Exodus, and the wandering in the desert. Certain Jews of Jesus' time, the Sadducees, accepted only these books as Scripture. They are still revered as the heart of the Scriptures in contemporary Judaism.

Genesis. This Greek title means "origin" or "beginning." The Book of Genesis has two distinct parts: chapters 1 to 11 speak of primeval history and serve as an introduction to the whole of the Hebrew Scriptures; chapters 12 to 50 tell the story of the ancient patriarchs Abraham, Isaac, Jacob, and Joseph, beginning with Abraham's call about 1800 B.C.

Genesis begins with two creation accounts. Both are statements of Israel's faith in God. Attempts to subject these imaginative descriptions to scientific scrutiny are misguided and misleading. The first creation account is from the Priestly tradition (written in the fifth century B.C.) and is a hymn of praise to the Creator. It shows evidence of the word-theology that emerged from the Exile in the writings of Second Isaiah (Is 40-55). The second account is from the Yahwist (tenth century B.C.) and demonstrates the down-to-earth storytelling gift of this writer. Both accounts stress the superiority of man and woman over other beings created by God.

The remaining chapters of the introductory section (1-11) describe humanity's sinful response to the bountiful Creator and the snowballing effects of sin in the world. Cain is infected, then Lamech (4), then all the world, so much so that God cleanses the world by the Flood. Sin begins to grow again immediately after the Flood (9) till it reaches a second climax at the Tower of Babel (11). This time, though, instead of wiping the world clean of sinners, God decides to work within human history through one of its families. Several of the stories and images of this introductory section are borrowed from the folklore of neighboring peoples, but infused with a new, inspired meaning.

The call of Abraham in chapter 12 marks the beginning of the "history of salvation." The stories about this patriarch reveal a man of his own time, not a superman, but a man led by faith in Yahweh. This faith is put to the ultimate test in the command to sacrifice Abraham and Sarah's only son, Isaac (22). The Isaac stories are very brief, a sort of interlude between Abraham and his colorful grandson, Jacob. The narratives about Jacob, who will be regarded as the father of the nation of Israel, are remarkably candid about the sins and flaws of this forefather. But this honesty makes the drama of his transformation that much more convincing.

The final chapters of the book (37-50) center around the fortunes of Jacob's favorite son, Joseph. The meaning of Israel's own history and life is subtly woven into the narratives of betrayal, fear, trust, and journey to an unknown land. The Joseph story takes the family of Abraham from Canaan into Egypt for Israel's formative experience of salvation: the scene is being set for the Hebrews' enslavement and liberation in the Exodus. At the end of the book they are dwelling peacefully in Egypt, and Joseph's bones are waiting in mummy wrapping for the return to the land of Israel (50:25-26).

Exodus. The Book of Exodus ("departure") begins with the description of Israel's slavery in Egypt about 1300 B.C. The early years of Moses, his call at the burning bush, and the beginning of the mission of Moses and Aaron carry the story up to the Ten Plagues and the confrontation with Pharaoh (7-11). Before leaving Egypt, the Israelites eat the Passover meal, the model for future celebrations. In the pivotal chapters 14 and 15, the crossing of the sea is portrayed in both prose and poetry as a mighty act of divine deliverance.

Moses leads the people from the sea through the desert to Mount Sinai amid much grumbling. The theme of murmuring is highlighted in the Book of Numbers. At Sinai, God appears to Moses and gives him the Code of the Covenant, containing the Ten Commandments, and the people seal their covenant with God in blood (19-24). Details of the construction of the desert sanctuary occupy thirteen of the remaining sixteen chapters. The other three chapters tell of the Israelites' worship of a golden calf and the renewal of the tablets of the Law.

Moses grows in stature as the narrative proceeds. First he is hesitant to accept the mission proclaimed to him by Yahweh. He foresees the harsh demands of a thankless task. But eventually his staunch fidelity grows and prevails. When he descends the mountain with the second set of tablets, Moses radiates God's own glory (34:29-35). God's presence among his people is symbolized by fire at night and a cloud during the day. The journey does not end with the completion of the Exodus. The fire and the cloud in the concluding verses imply that the journey is still going on, even for readers many generations later, and God is still with his people.

Leviticus. This book was put into its present form as a guide for religious observance in the post-exilic community. It contains various laws, customs, and ceremonies used in the exercise of the Levitical priesthood. (All the service of the sanctuary was assigned to the tribe of Levi.) Though the instructions are presented as communicated through Moses during the wilderness period, they were actually formulated at later times. The Jerusalem priests compiled the earliest part of the book, the

Holiness Code (17-26), around 600 B.C. Other parts were added during the Babylonian Exile, and the work was amended and put into its final form in the fifth century B.C.

Chapters 1-7 present laws governing cultic sacrifice; Leviticus 8-10 describes the installation of Aaron and his sons as priests. Then follow laws of ritual purity (11-15) and directions for the Day of Atonement (16). The holiness code (17-26) contains more purity laws and directives for the great feasts and the holy years. The book ends with an appendix (27) on votive offerings which modifies some of the laws in the light of later practice.

Numbers. Numbers continues the historical narrative of the Book of Exodus, tracing the wandering of the people from Sinai to the Promised Land of Canaan. Chapters describing various ritual and social laws are interspersed throughout the narrative. The name of the book derives from the two censuses of the Hebrew people in chapters 1-4 and 26. Many of the legal prescriptions date from a much later time in Israel, when the Israelites were established in the land and no longer nomadic. Numbers also contains materials with an archaic flavor, like the trial by ordeal for a woman charged with adultery (Nm 5), in which primitive belief in the power of a curse is graphically demonstrated.

The journey narrative follows and supplements the Book of Exodus beginning with chapter 9. The Israelites celebrate their second Passover, the first outside Egypt. They move from Sinai amid continual grumbling. Moses shares his leadership with seventy elders (Nm 11). Later the Jewish Sanhedrin will consist of seventy elders plus the high priest in imitation of this structure. Highlights of the journey stories in Numbers are the scouting of the Promised Land (Nm 13-14), the rebellion of Korah (16), and the adventures of Balaam (22-24). Chapter 35 explains the institution of "cities of refuge," where accidental homicides might find protection in an era when private vengeance was often the rule.

Deuteronomy. This Greek name means literally "second law"; it is derived from the Greek translation of the words "copy of this law" in Deuteronomy 17:18. The Book of Deuteronomy is composed as a "last testament" of Moses at the end of the desert wandering. He speaks to the people on the plains of Moab east of the Jordan River, where the people are poised for their entry into the Promised Land. His words issue a vigorous call to the people to keep the Law faithfully. He reviews many of the laws already recorded and recalls various episodes of the desert wandering. After blessing the twelve tribes, Moses dies and is buried.

The core of this book, which has been edited and amended over centuries, is the law code in chapters 12 to 26. This, or some part of it, seems to have been the "book of the law" (2 Kgs 22:8) which formed the basis for the reform under King Josiah (622 B.C.). Deuteronomy is one of the most homiletic and theological books in the Old Testament. The dominant theological ideas of the Deuteronomist school include the election (God's choice) of the Israelites, their duty to remain pure in observance, especially shunning idolatry, the worship of Yahweh by sacrifice in Jerusalem exclusively, joy in serving the Lord, and confidence in his authority and power.

Deuteronomy is the source of the traditional Shema prayer (named after its first word in Hebrew: "Hear!"), recited by faithful Jews morning and evening over the centuries, a formula Christians recognize as the Great Commandment (6:4-5; Mk 12:29-30). The book also preserves the Ten Commandments in a form somewhat different from that in Exodus (5:6-21; compare Ex 20:2-17). Moses' blessing upon the twelve tribes (33) contains reflections of various stages of Israelite history.

Prophets

This section in the Hebrew Bible is subdivided into Former Prophets and Latter Prophets. Most of the figures we associate with prophecy (Isaiah, Jeremiah, Ezekiel, etc.) belong to the Latter Prophets collection. The Former Prophets are historical books: Joshua, Judges, 1 and 2 Samuel, and 1 and 2 Kings. These were looked on as "prophets" because of the prominent action of figures like Samuel, Elijah, and Elisha in these narratives. Scholars today refer to the Former Prophets collection as the Deuteronomic History, so called after the school of writers who compiled these narratives (early sixth century B.C.) in light of the principles enunciated in the Book of Deuteronomy.

Former Prophets

Joshua. The torch of Moses passes to his assistant, Joshua, in chapter 1. Then the book tells of the conquest of Canaan (2-12) and its division (13-21). The narratives present a highly idealized picture of the taking of the land and illustrate strong theological ideas. There is a liturgical flair to the various ceremonies accompanying the crossing of the Jordan and the conquering of cities like Jericho. Readers often have trouble with the contemporary morality that insisted on the total annihilation of enemy cities and populations. This practice was an inheritance from barbarous times which was gradually purged as God led the Hebrews to a deeper moral sensitivity.

Chapter 23 is a plea of Joshua, in his old age, for fidelity to the covenant (reminiscent of Moses in Deuteronomy); chapter 24 contains the famous scene of the renewal of the covenant at Shechem, when Joshua challenged the people with the words: "As for me and my household, we will serve the Lord" (24:15).

Judges. The Book of Judges covers the period between the conquest of the land and the establishment of the monarchy (1250-1050 B.C.), when Israel was ruled by local chieftains. After an opening chapter describing various traditions of local settlement, the theme is set in chapter 2: the people were provided with "judges," or leaders, to lead them as long as they were faithful to the Lord; but when they sinned, they experienced hostility and suffering. Then they called out to the Lord and he heard their prayer.

The major judges in this book are Othniel, Ehud, Deborah (with Barak), Gideon, Abimelech, Jephthah, and Samson. The canticle of Deborah (Jgs 5) is one of the oldest pieces of literature in the Bible. The story of Gideon shows Israel at a settled agricultural stage, unable to protect itself against the desert raiders coming with camels, animals capable of swift travel over long distances. The end of the story of Gideon shows the hostility toward monarchs that will fire the debates at the time of Saul's accession (Jgs 8:22-23; 1 Sm 8). The judges are not always paragons of virtue or good judgment (for example, Jephthah, Samson), but they are heroes who helped Israel carve out its unique niche in the ancient world.

1 and 2 Samuel. First and Second Samuel were originally a single book. The Greek translators divided it into two and were followed in this by the Latin and all subsequent translators. Not only did they divide the book, the Greek translators gave the parts a new name, 1 and 2 Kingdoms, which became 1 and 2 Kings in the Latin version. This led to a confusion of names in the past, when Catholic Bibles entitled 1 and 2 Samuel "1 and 2 Kings" and entitled 1 and 2 Kings as "3 and 4 Kings." All recent Bibles, however, refer to the present books as 1 and 2 Samuel and reserve the title "1 and 2 Kings" for the following books.

First Samuel narrates the birth and call of the prophet Samuel, his leadership as judge, and his hesitant participation in the creation of a monarchy. The middle chapters relate the transition to the rule of Saul, the first king, and his dealings with Samuel. The last part of the book describes the rise of David and his interactions with Saul. Samuel's death is recorded in chapter 25, Saul's in chapter 31. An early story of the Ark of the Covenant is contained in chapters 4 to 7.

Samuel himself does not appear at all in 2 Samuel. It is the story of the transition of the rule from Saul to David, with David's military victories and his unification of the kingdom. Chapters 9 to 20 give an early, probably eyewitness, account of the family history of David, recounting some of the most colorful tales associated with the great king. The book concludes with an appendix of four chapters of historical fragments.

1 and 2 Kings. The books of 1 and 2 Kings, like 1 and 2 Samuel, were originally a single work. The first two chapters of 1 Kings continue the family history of David, describing his death and preparing for the accession of Solomon. Solomon's history is told in chapters 3 to 11. The division of the kingdom under Rehoboam is described in chapter 12. The rest of the book follows the history of the divided kingdom, concluding with the first stories of Elijah and his confrontations with King Ahab and Queen Jezebel.

Second Kings continues the history of the kingdoms until the fall of Israel (17), and more stories of Elijah. The stories of his successor, Elisha, begin in chapter 2 and continue until the description of Elisha's death in chapter 13. Chapters 18 to 25 follow the last years of Judah until the fall of Jerusalem in 587 B.C.

Latter Prophets

This collection is made up of the three major prophets: Isaiah, Jeremiah, and Ezekiel, and the group called "The Twelve," or Minor Prophets: Hosea, Joel, Amos, Obadiah, Jonah, Micah, Nahum, Habbakuk, Zephaniah, Haggai, Zechariah, and Malachi.

Isaiah. The book is conveniently divided into two main parts, chapters 1 to 39 and 40 to 66. The first part is associated with the prophet Isaiah, who lived in Jerusalem and carried on a prophetic mission from 742 B.C. until at least 701. It was a time of much tension because of the threats of Assyria. During Isaiah's time the northern kingdom was captured and many inhabitants were taken into exile (721 B.C.), and Jerusalem itself was under siege (701).

Isaiah's ministry may be divided into three periods coinciding with the reigns of Kings Jotham (742-735 B.C.), Ahaz (735-715 B.C.), and Hezekiah (715-687 B.C.). Because he served as advisor to the kings, Isaiah's book contains court intrigue. Isaiah warned about the moral breakdown in Judah during all three periods, but it was only Hezekiah who undertook a religious reform. Even he was not strong enough in faith to rely consistently on the Lord. Chapters 36 to 39 are a historical appendix (taken from 2 Kings 18-20), describing the advance of Sennacherib on Jerusalem in 701 B.C.

The poems in these early chapters were recorded after Isaiah's death. Most of them come from the prophet himself, but some of them were composed in his spirit by later disciples. One famous later section is the so-called Apocalypse of Isaiah (24-27). The call of Isaiah is recorded in the beautiful scene in the Temple in chapter 6, where the prophet is overawed by the vision of Yahweh enthroned in glory. Isaiah offers himself for the mission but must first have his lips cleansed in order to proclaim the word of God. Other notable passages are the Song of the Vineyard (5:1-7) and the Book of Immanuel (6-9) containing the messianic oracles familiar in the Advent and Christmas liturgy.

Chapters 40 to 55 are known today as "Second Isaiah" because they derive from a different person, an unknown prophet of the Babylonian Exile (587-538 B.C.). In these chapters the prophet consoles the exiles and promises a return to Israel that will be like a new Exodus. The prophet sees Cyrus, the Persian liberator of the Hebrews, as God's Messiah (45:1). This section also contains the four Servant Songs (42:1-4; 49:1-6; 50:4-9; 52:13-53:12). A figure identified as the "Servant of Yahweh" is portrayed as endowed with a mission of bringing forth righteousness in the whole world. He is opposed, suffers, and is even put to death, but Yahweh brings his work to fruition. The fourth song describes his death as a sin offering bringing forgiveness: "by his stripes we were healed" (53:5).

This song was used by New Testament writers to interpret the death and resurrection of Jesus. The concluding chapters 56 to 66 contain prophetic oracles from the postexilic period.

Jeremiah. Jeremiah received his prophetic call in 626 B.C. and exercised it faithfully until he disappeared from history in 587, taken by force into Egypt at the time of the Babylonian Exile. The book, compiled after his death, contains many prophetic oracles, but especially striking is the great amount of biographical material that makes Jeremiah the prophet we know best as a person.

Only the Book of Psalms is longer than Jeremiah among the books of the Bible. For some unexplained reason, the Greek translation is about one eighth shorter than the Hebrew text. The first twenty chapters contain oracles in generally chronological order; chapters 21 to 25 contain oracles from various periods; chapters 26 to 45 are mostly biographical; chapters 46 to 51 contain oracles against the nations; chapter 52 is a historical appendix taken from 2 Kings 24 to 25.

A special feature are the five "confessions" of Jeremiah, personal prayers which probably were not intended for publication (11:18-12:6; 15:10-21; 17:14-18; 18:18-23; 20:7-18). From these and other personal glimpses, such as the vocation of Jeremiah (1:6), we get the picture of a reluctant prophet whose faithful dedication to his ministry brought him suffering, ostracism, and exile (43:6). There were conspiracies against his life; for announcing the destruction of the Temple he was tried for blasphemy; for announcing the destruction of the city of Jerusalem he was placed in the stocks (20:2). In order to be a living sign that families would not survive the punishment of Israel (16:1-4), he did not marry.

Jeremiah had very pained relations with Jehoiakim and Zedekiah, the two kings who ruled most of the last twenty-two years before the Exile. In a vivid court scene, Jehoiakim listened to the reading of the prophecies of Jeremiah, cutting away the columns of the scroll as they were finished and casting them into the fire (36:23). Zedekiah was well-meaning but weak. During the latter days of Zedekiah's reign, Jeremiah spent time on one occasion in a dungeon and on another in a cistern (37-38). According to tradition he was put to death by his own countrymen in Egypt.

Ezekiel. In contrast to Jeremiah, we know very little about Ezekiel. His writings reveal that he was a priest exiled to Babylon with the first wave of deportees in 597 B.C. The early part of his career, reflected in chapters 1 to 24, was a mission of warning about Jerusalem's impending doom. The glory of the Lord would depart from the Temple if there were no signs of repentance. This section (and the book) begins with the memorable vision of the Lord in his chariot-throne. Ezekiel describes his prophetic call as an experience of consuming the word of God in the form of a scroll (3:1-4). Ezekiel's prophecy of the destruction of Jerusalem was vindicated by the events of 587 B.C.; after this his message becomes one of hope for the future. In the midst of exile the prophet proclaims a vision of restoration. Ezekiel foretells Israel's rise from the death of exile in Babylon to new life in the famous vision of the dry bones (37).

Chapters 25 to 32 contain oracles against the nations; chapters 33 to 38, prophecies of restoration after the fall of Jerusalem; chapters 40 to 48, a mystical description of the renewed city and its Temple. Ezekiel is unique for the number of his visions, and for his many symbolic actions, such as shaving, burning, and dividing his hair (5:1-4), and pantomiming the actions of the exiles (12:1-20). It is doubtful that Ezekiel himself was alive to share in the return to Jerusalem, but through his prophecy he had enormous influence on the life of post-exilic Judah.

Minor Prophets

The prophets represented by these twelve books are called "minor" only because of the brevity of their written collections. Several of them were major prophetic figures of their own time, for example, Hosea, Amos, Haggai, and Zechariah. They are treated here in the order of their appearance in the Hebrew Bible (the order of most English Bibles) which is not chronological. Because history is important in the study of the prophets, the order of their appearance in Israelite history is indicated by numbers after their names.

Hosea (2). Hosea began prophesying in the northern kingdom (Israel) about 750 B.C., toward the end of the long and prosperous reign of Jeroboam II (786-746). Hosea warns against the moral softness which accompanied the growth of prosperity, typified in neglect of the poor and by the adoption of superstitions and even idolatrous worship practices from the Canaanites. Hosea was the first prophet to compare the relationship of Yahweh to Israel with that of a husband and wife. His vocation was not only to proclaim the message of God's love but to image it in his own life. He married the unfaithful Gomer, humbling himself again and again to take her back as his wife.

The book falls into two distinct parts: chapters 1 to 3, which contain the prophet's autobiographical account of his marriage and its application to the situation of Israel; and chapters 4 to 14, a collection of oracles detailing Israel's infidelities and warning her of the consequences. His warning was verified a few years later in the Assyrian takeover of Israel (721 B.C.). A favorite among these later chapters is chapter 11, which portrays Yahweh as a loving parent pondering the waywardness of his child, Israel.

Joel (11). Joel prophesied 350 years after Hosea among drastically changed conditions. The date was about 400 B.C., long after the return of the exiles from Babylon to Judah. The people had responded positively to the reforming work of Nehemiah and Ezra. The Temple worship was being performed faithfully and well. But the land was being ravaged by a terrible locust invasion, a scourge so harsh that it aroused fear that the end was coming—if not the end of the world, the death of many of the people.

Joel used the locust invasion as an image of the day of judgment, the "day of the Lord" (2:1), and called the people to prayer and penance. The people responded, the Lord heard their prayer, and disaster was averted. Joel's short book is a prophetic call to the people up to 2:17; after this the message is one of blessings for God's people and judgment on the nations. Verse discrepancies are sometimes a problem with this book because the Greek (and Latin) translators combined chapter 3 with chapter 2. Modern translations follow the Hebrew division of four chapters.

Amos (1). Amos prophesied a few years earlier than Hosea (beginning about 760 B.C.) during the reign of Jeroboam II in the north. Though he was a native of the southern kingdom of Judah, Amos proclaimed his warnings in Israel, much to the chagrin of officials there. He possessed a very strong sense of divine vocation as a nonprofessional called from being "a shepherd and a dresser of sycamores" (7:14) to fulfill a special mission for the Lord. Amos' book is a collection of oracles against the nations and warnings to Israel and Judah. Like Hosea, he calls attention to the social injustice which makes worship a travesty.

Obadiah (10). This is the shortest book among the Hebrew Scriptures, and the harshest prophecy. Written toward the end of the fifth century B.C., it reflects the ancient enmity between Israel and Edom, a neighbor to the southeast. Edom had applauded the downfall of Jerusalem and the Temple nearly two centuries earlier, and now this unknown prophet gloats over the Edomites' forced departure from their own land. He also warns of a coming judgment and foresees a future when Yahweh will be king in a purified Israel.

Jonah (12). The Book of Jonah is different from the other prophetic writings in that it is a narrative describing the prophet and his work rather than recording his message. Today the book is recognized as a parable confronting the Jews of postexilic times with their own narrowness toward other peoples. Jonah is sent to preach to the pagan Ninevites against his will and is indignant when they repent and turn to the Lord. The anonymous author is urging an awareness of and openness to the promise of universal salvation given through Abraham (Gn 12:1-3).

Micah (3). Micah was a contemporary of Isaiah of Jerusalem (late eighth century B.C.) and also preached in Judah. He is in the central prophetic tradition of calling the people back to true observance of the Law and pure worship and warning of destruction if the plea is not heard. He witnessed the fall of Samaria (721 B.C.) and the advance of the Assyrian Sennacherib on Jerusalem in 701 B.C. He is the first prophet to envisage the fall of Jerusalem (3:12). Micah's oracle about Bethlehem as the Messiah's place of origin (5:1) is cited in the New Testament (Mt 2:6; Jn 7:42).

Nahum (5). This book resembles Obadiah in its exultation over God's judgment on a hated enemy. Assyria threatened and scourged God's people for two hundred years. But in 612 B.C. the Babylonians and Medes toppled Assyria and its capital city of Nineveh. Nahum prophesied shortly before the fall of Nineveh, focusing on the justice of God.

Habbakuk (6). Habbakuk's prophecy dates from the time of the crushing advance of Babylon toward Jerusalem which occurred between 605 and 587 B.C. Thus he, like Zephaniah and Nahum, was a contemporary of Jeremiah. Habbakuk, like Jeremiah, questions the Lord about his divine management of affairs: a wicked nation is about to engulf the chosen people. Habbakuk receives the explanation that God is using Babylon as an instrument of justice and that the just among the Israelites will not perish. The short book ends with a magnificent statement of faith in spite of adversity.

Zephaniah (4). Zephaniah prophesied during the early years of King Josiah (640-609 B.C.), but before the introduction of the reforms of 621. He condemned the corruption that arose during the reigns of kings Manasseh (687-642 B.C.) and Amon (642-640 B.C.), particularly the introduction of idolatry and superstition into the worship of Yahweh. Zephaniah's ministry reflected the influence of Amos and Isaiah and served as an influence on his contemporary, Jeremiah. His book is a collection of oracles against pagan nations and warnings for Jerusalem, closing with a promise of final deliverance for God's people.

Haggai (7). Haggai and Zechariah sought to rouse the exiles returned from Babylon into an active campaign to rebuild the Temple. The Jews who returned had laid the foundation on their arrival in 538 B.C., but their enthusiasm had waned in the struggle for survival among hostile neighbors and in a ruined city. They had built their own homes but not the Temple during the next two decades. Haggai began a vigorous campaign in late August 520 B.C., and by the end of his recorded ministry four months later saw the renewal of construction work. His book contains the three oracles at the beginning, middle, and end of this period.

Haggai addressed his message from the Lord to the two pillars of the postexilic community, Zerubbabel the governor and Joshua the high priest. The beginning of his preaching is dated precisely to the first day of the sixth month of the second year of Darius I, the Persian ruler (521-486 B.C.). The shake-up of the empire after the death of Cambyses II (528-522 B.C.) inspired some of the subordinate states to strike for independence. Haggai may have suggested independence for Judah (2:22-23), but his main message is the revival of the spiritual heritage through the construction of a new Temple. His second oracle fell on the Feast of Booths (2:1), a time when the deepest religious and national sentiments of the people could be aroused.

Zechariah (8). Zechariah's prophetic ministry began two months later than Haggai's in 520 B.C. His book records the series of visions he received three months later and a final oracle given in November 518 B.C. These messages urged continued work on the Temple and promised a future glory for Jerusalem. Neither Haggai nor Zechariah record the successful outcome of their mission, the dedication of the new Temple in 515 B.C. (Ezr 6:15-16).

Zechariah's collection opens with a brief oracle calling for a conversion in the classical prophetic tradition (1:3; compare Hos 6:1). The second and central oracle, given months later (January and February 519 B.C.) consists of a series of eight visions. This section, beginning with the vision of the four horsemen (1:7-17), later had significant influence on the Book of Revelation. Zechariah foresaw the downfall of Israel's enemies. The Babylonians would be punished while Jerusalem would blossom into a city too large for its walls (2:4-9). An appendix after the eighth vision (6:9-15) is an interesting example of the editing of a text to fit new circumstances. Zerubbabel's name was replaced by Joshua's (verse 11) when Persia halted the line of kings, to scotch any idea of a renewal of the Davidic kingdom.

Like the Book of Isaiah, Zechariah is a composite containing, besides the prophet's own utterances, writings from a much later period. Chapters 9 to 14 refer to events that occurred at least two hundred years later. The overthrow of the Persians by Alexander the Great in 333 B.C. is the backdrop for some of the oracles in this latter part of the book. In fact, the march of Yahweh through Syria, Lebanon, and Palestine in chapter 9 is patterned on the triumphant campaign of Alexander after his decisive defeat of the Persians on the Plain of Issus.

The interests of the later chapters are different from those in chapters 1 to 8. These poems foresee the establishment of a new messianic age and show dependence on the prophecy of Joel made about 400 B.C. A new kind of royal messianism is present: no longer the expectation of a glorious Davidic kingdom under a warrior-prince Messiah; the Messiah will make a more humble appearance when he comes as Jerusalem's just Savior (9:9-10). This second half of Zechariah was a favorite source for Jesus and the evangelists. Jesus consciously dramatized one of the prophetic scenes in making his triumphal entry into Jerusalem (9:9; Mt 21:5; Jn 12:15).

Malachi (9). This prophet received his call a little more than half a century after the completion of the second Temple. His prophecy dates to around 450 B.C. The worship of Yahweh had been provided for materially in the construction of the Temple, but abuses crept into the worship to ruin the spiritual dimension. Malachi issued stern warnings and criticism to the priests. He was laying the groundwork for the reforming mission of Nehemiah and Ezra which began a few years later.

Malachi records six distinct messages in a challenging series of dialogues. Statements by Yahweh or the prophet are followed by questions from the listeners and then by prophetic responses. One of his oracles interprets halfhearted worship as sneering at the Lord (1:6-7). Another makes a brilliant application of covenant theology to the bond of marriage (2:10-16). The prophet foresaw universal salvation culminating in worldwide sacrificial worship of Yahweh (1:11). Malachi's image of the messenger sent to prepare the way to the Temple for Yahweh (3:1-3) was applied to John the Baptist in the Gospels (Mk 1:2).

SEVEN

The Hebrew Scriptures II:
Writings

The third general category of books in the Hebrew Bible, the "Writings," is the least homogeneous of the collections. It simply contains all the inspired literature, generally late in appearance, which was not included in the Law and Prophets. The first reference to the threefold division is in the foreword to the Book of Sirach (Ecclesiasticus) written by the author's grandson around 130 B.C.: "Many important truths have been handed down to us through the Law, the prophets, and the later authors; and for these the instruction and wisdom of Israel merit praise." Our treatment will organize these remaining books into the prophetic, the historical, and the sapiential.

Other Prophetic Literature

The three books treated under this heading span 500 years of Israel's history. All are anonymous but have been connected to the names of great figures of the past.

Lamentations. In most English Bibles, Lamentations follows the Book of Jeremiah, and in some Bibles, the book is entitled "The Lamentations of Jeremiah" after the trend set by the

Greek translators in 200 B.C. We know now that Jeremiah was not the author because of discrepancies in thought, terminology, and style with his authentic writings. But it is easy to see why the book was attributed to him. It was written in Jerusalem soon after the city's destruction by the Babylonians (587 B.C.) as foretold by Jeremiah, and the interpretation of the tragedy as punishment for the sins of the people echoes the utterances of the prophet.

The Hebrew Bible situates this book among the Writings instead of the Prophets, and in a group of five books called *Megilloth* or "Scrolls" which were designated by the rabbis for use on five important Jewish feasts. The books appear in the calendar order of their liturgical use: Song of Songs (Passover, spring), Ruth (Pentecost, early summer), Lamentations (Ninth of Ab, summer), Ecclesiastes (Tabernacles, fall), and Esther (Purim, winter). The ninth day of the month of Ab is a day of mourning for the national calamities suffered in the two Temple destructions by the Babylonians and the Romans.

The book consists of five lamentations (coinciding with the five chapters) over the loss of Jerusalem and the Temple. There is a progression of moods rather than of thought. Wave after wave of desolation rolls over the reader. In the first lamentation a visitor to the ruined city ponders the tragic reversal from beauty to misery; then Jerusalem speaks in her own name of her desolation. The second lamentation is by a citizen of Jerusalem. The third lamentation, the centerpiece of the book, expresses the pain of an average citizen of Jerusalem, a "man who knows affliction" (Lam 3:1). After the peak in chapter 3, the fourth lamentation returns to a mood similar to that of chapter 1, with a reporter giving a more objective picture of the city. In the fifth lamentation, the shortest, the inhabitants of Jerusalem address

Yahweh directly. Because of its different tenor, the fifth lamentation was entitled "The Prayer of Jeremiah" in the Latin Vulgate and "A Prayer" in some of the Greek versions.

A notable feature of Lamentations is the acrostic device employed by the author. Each chapter has twenty-two verses, the number of letters in the Hebrew alphabet. In chapters 1 through 4 each verse begins with a different letter of the alphabet in order. As a visual emphasis of the importance of chapter 3, all three lines of each verse begin with the same letter.

Daniel. The Book of Daniel was written during the Maccabean Revolt precipitated by the oppression of Antiochus IV Epiphanes between the years 167 and 164 B.C. It is crisis literature, which gives hope to sufferers of persecution. The author inspires confidence in God's providence by showing that events have been following a predetermined course for several hundred years. The present time of suffering, too, is part of God's plan and will have a happy conclusion.

The author built his story around Daniel, a young Hebrew taken into the royal household during the Babylonian Exile 400 years earlier (587-538 B.C.). There he distinguishes himself for dream interpretation and prophecy and is protected by the Hebrew God, Yahweh, from death in the lions' den. His visions provide a foreshadowing of the succession of empires between the Exile and the Maccabean era. Daniel foresees a resurrection of just and unjust at the end of the world (12:1-3), the earliest expression of such a vision in Hebrew literature.

The book's complicated history is reflected in the present text. Chapters 1 and 8 to 12 are written in Hebrew, 2 to 7 in Aramaic, and 13 and 14 in Greek. Three sections of Daniel are deuterocanonical (see chapter 4) and found only in Catholic

Bibles: 3:24-90, the prayer of Azariah and the song of the three young men; chapter 13, the story of Susanna; and chapter 14, Daniel's victories over the idol Bel and the dragon, and the mission of Habbakuk to Daniel in the lions' den. These stories were originally written in Hebrew or Aramaic but have come to the Bible in their Greek translation.

Chapters 1 to 4 portray Daniel's adventures during the time of Nebuchadnezzar, the Babylonian ruler who destroyed Jerusalem and began the Exile of the Jews. Chapter 5 takes place during the reign of Belshazzar, who is presented as the son of Nebuchadnezzar. This framework is one of the clues to the imaginative character of the work. Belshazzar was never the king of Babylon, nor was he the son of Nebuchadnezzar. He was the son of Nabonidus, the last king of Babylon before the Persian takeover. In chapter 6, Daniel is harassed by the new Persian king, Darius the Mede, a figure unknown to history.

The most familiar section of the book to readers of the New Testament is chapters 7 to 13, which contain the apocalyptic visions of the future. The mission of the Son of Man coming on the clouds of heaven is evoked in Jesus' words before the Sanhedrin (Dn 7:13-14; Mk 14:62). The Book of Revelation alludes to the Ancient of Days (Dn 7:22; Rv 1:14), Michael the great prince (Dn 10:13; Rv 12:7-12), and the four beasts (Dn 7; Rv 13:1-2).

Baruch. The Book of Baruch, also set in the Babylonian Exile, was put into its present form around 50 B.C., though some of its contents date back to more than a hundred years earlier. Judah had recently lost its independence to the Romans and fear arose that the people would be absorbed by the Hellenistic culture and forget the unique tradition for which their ancestors struggled so valiantly. The author sought to rouse his fellow Jews to a sense of their historic roots.

The author pictured Baruch, the secretary of Jeremiah, ministering to the needs of the exiles in Babylon. He leads them in days of prayer and fasting and in remembering Jerusalem. The narrative section is followed by beautiful poems in praise of wisdom (3:9-4:4) and in encouragement of the exiles (4:5-5:9). Chapter 6, the letter of Jeremiah to the exiles, was originally a separate text warning Jews of the Diaspora against idolatry. Baruch is one of the deuterocanonical books of the Catholic Bible.

Later Historical Books

Some of the books under this title are historical only in the sense that they feature persons or situations from Israel's past.

Ruth. The story of Ruth, set in the time of Judges, is based on the tradition that one of David's ancestors was a foreigner from Moab. A Hebrew couple, Elimelech and Naomi, had migrated to Moab in a time of famine. Elimelech and their two sons died in a ten-year period. Naomi decides to return to Palestine and advises her two daughters-in-law to find new husbands in their native Moab. But Ruth expresses a desire to remain with Naomi in filial loyalty: "Wherever you go I will go, wherever you lodge I will lodge, your people shall be my people, and your God my God" (1:16). Ruth accompanies Naomi to Palestine and eventually marries the influential Boaz of Bethlehem; they become the great-grandparents of David.

The book is postexilic, written probably around 400 B.C. It challenged the narrow perspective of Judah in the wake of the reforms of Nehemiah and Ezra, when national fervor encouraged intolerance of foreigners, and marriages between Jews and gentiles were dissolved. Ruth is mentioned in the family tree of Jesus (Mt 1:5). In the Jewish liturgy this book is read on the feast of Pentecost.

1 and 2 Chronicles. The two books of Chronicles and the books of Ezra and Nehemiah originally formed a single historical work written not long after 400 B.C. In old Catholic Bibles, 1 and 2 Chronicles appear as 1 and 2 Paralipomenon because the Latin Vulgate simply transliterated the Greek title which means "leftovers" or things omitted from the earlier books of Samuel and Kings. This title is not an accurate statement of the contents of the two books, which repeat many of the historical events narrated earlier. What the Chronicler does is rather to select information from these sources and others and give it a careful, new, theological interpretation.

A new set of circumstances demanded a new theological interpretation. It became clear that the past political glory of Israel was irretrievably lost. The returnees from exile possessed fleeting hopes of a renewed Davidic dynasty beginning with Zerubbabel, but this vision was shattered by the Persian overlords by 500 B.C. Now, more than a hundred years later, Judah needed a new sense of purpose. The Chronicler recognized the crucial importance of the centrality of Temple worship in Jerusalem; infidelity to worship had provoked the earlier downfall. Linked to Jerusalem worship in the Chronicler's mind was reverence for the Davidic dynasty and the divine promises associated with it.

The Chronicler idealized the history of David's Israel. He omitted the intrigues and many of the battles recorded in the books of Samuel and Kings. David is presented as a second

Moses, authorizing the elaborate Temple ritual and appointing Levites to coordinate the liturgical program. The remark has been made that David, in Chronicles, has become a "royal sacristan."

The first ten chapters of 1 Chronicles trace Hebrew genealogies from Adam (the first word of the book) to David. The author does not include information about Moses and Aaron which might diminish the importance of David. The rest of the book, chapters 11 to 29, are devoted to the history of David. Though David is told by the prophet Nathan that the Temple is not to be built by David but by his son Solomon (17:11-12; 2 Sm 7:13), David is presented as gathering materials for the building (22:2-5). Israel's ideal king must be responsible for the Temple.

Solomon's reign and the building of the Temple cover the first quarter (1-9) of 2 Chronicles. The author omits the hostile commentary of 1 Kings 11 on Solomon's sinfulness. After the description of the split of the monarchy (10-12), the bulk of the book (13-36) tells the history of the kingdom of Judah until its demise in 587 B.C. The final word, though, is one of hope: the decrees of Cyrus the Persian for the return to Jerusalem and the rebuilding of the Temple (36:22-23). The Chronicler ignores the history of the northern kingdom and omits northern figures like Elijah and Elisha.

Ezra and Nehemiah. The books of Ezra and Nehemiah derive from a single work, which is why the mission of Ezra appears in both books. They were called 1 and 2 Esdras in Catholic Bibles translated from the Latin Vulgate. This does not explain, however, why the material in the work, whether one document or two, is so jumbled. The books do not contain a chronological arrangement. The reader may find reassurance in knowing this from the beginning. The division into two books occurred in the early Christian centuries and was eventually accepted in the Hebrew Bible in the fifteenth century.

Ezra and Nehemiah provide the most important sources for the history of the development of Judaism after the Exile. The historical overview in chapter 5 of this handbook adopts the following sequence of events during the period covered by Ezra-Nehemiah.

Nehemiah received his commission to restore the walls of Jerusalem in 445 B.C. He completed this work and remained as governor for twelve years until he was apparently called back to Persia. He received a second commission a year or two later, during which time he corrected Temple abuses and created strict laws against intermarriage with foreigners. Ezra came to Jerusalem some time after Nehemiah (how soon is disputed). He called the people back to faithful practice of the whole ancient religion, giving them the Book of the Law and enforcing even stricter marriage laws than those of Nehemiah. Under his leadership, the people ratified the covenant again.

The Chronicler used a number of original source documents to tell the story of Ezra and Nehemiah. It is fairly certain that some sections are personal accounts from the two leaders themselves (Ezr 7:12-9:15; Neh 1:1-7:5). The section containing the documents from the Persian archives in Ezra 4:8-7:28 is written in Aramaic instead of Hebrew. The books contain lists of returnees from exile and of the population of Jerusalem. The author probably had some difficulty, more than a hundred years after the events, in knowing just how these various documents related to one another.

The Chronicler begins the Book of Ezra by repeating the

verses that were placed at the end of 2 Chronicles concerning Cyrus' decree ending the Exile. The earlier Israelite historian, the Deuteronomist author, recorded the history of the people up to the Exile. The Chronicler extends the story to the following century, but omits any discussion of the Exile. He bypasses it to describe the new beginning under Sheshbazzar, Zerubbabel, and Joshua. The first six chapters of Ezra record the return to Jerusalem, the struggle against the Samaritans over the rebuilding of the Temple, and the successful completion of the Temple under the urging of Haggai and Zechariah. Then follow the history of Ezra's mission to Jerusalem and a list of the people who accompanied him (Ezr 7-8), his dispute with the Jews who had married foreign women, and a list of the offenders (Ezr 9-10).

The Book of Nehemiah begins with Nehemiah's own report of his commission to restore Jerusalem's walls. Nehemiah makes his journey to Judah, examines the city walls, and plans to rebuild them in spite of Samaritan opposition (Neh 2). A list probably drawn up after the work was done is inserted as chapter 3. Chapters 4 to 6 give a very lively and intimate account of the work of building and of the interference of the opposition. A portrait of Nehemiah emerges from these chapters: a man of faith, single-minded in his dedication to serving God's people. Chapter 7 repeats the census report of the inhabitants of Judah given in Ezra 2.

The census and the proclamation of the Law by Ezra are placed after the completion of the wall (Neh 8-9) to give the impression that Ezra's ministry followed immediately. But this act of renewal probably came several years later. The concluding chapters (Neh 10-13) return to the time of Nehemiah. These describe the signing of a sealed pact (Neh 10), the plan for repopulating Jerusalem (Neh 11), the dedication of the new wall (Neh 12), and the institution of religious reforms (Neh 13).

Tobit. This book and the two following differ greatly from the work of the Chronicler. They are interpretations of the history of Israel, but they fit better under the rubric of religious novel than of religious history. Tobit is a deuterocanonical book written in Aramaic in the second or third century B.C. The text came to us through its Greek translation and only recently have fragments of the book in its original language been discovered near the Dead Sea. Like the Book of Esther, Tobit gives a picture of Jewish life in the Diaspora. The setting is historical, but the characters and the story are not.

A faithful and wealthy Israelite, Tobit lived in the northern kingdom at the time of its fall in 721 B.C. He and his wife, Anna, and their son, Tobiah, were deported to Assyria to live in the capital city of Nineveh. The story takes place there during the reigns of Assyrian rulers Shalmaneser V, Sennacherib, and Esarhaddon. Its theme is the triumph of virtue. Tobit suffers several trials, including living as a fugitive because of his good deeds and being blinded, but good fortune always returns. The longest section of the book (4-12) tells of Tobiah's quest for his wife, Sarah, and of his protection and ultimate success because of the assistance of the angel Raphael who accompanied him in disguise.

Judith. The Book of Judith proclaims Yahweh's care for his people and urges fidelity to the Law and trust in his protection in times of danger. It is a deuterocanonical book from the late second century B.C. when the Jews were struggling against the hellenizing pressures of the Seleucids. The story is set in the period after the Babylonian Exile, shortly after the rebuilding of the Temple (515 B.C.). The author seems purposely to leave clues that reveal the fictional nature of his story. The enemy ruler is "Nebuchadnezzar, king of the Assyrians in the great city of Nineveh" (1:1). But Nebuchadnezzar was a Babylonian king in whose time Nineveh lay in ruins (in fact, it was destroyed by Nebuchadnezzar's grandfather). This king is credited with the conquest of Ecbatana (1:14) which was actually taken by Cyrus the Persian. The story takes place in the imaginary Israelite city of Bethulia (4:6). In this context, the name of the heroine, which means "Jewess," is evidently symbolic.

In the story of Judith, King Nebuchadnezzar intends to punish a number of small nations because of their refusal to aid him in a war against the Medes. His general Holofernes besieges the Jews in Bethulia for thirty-four days, cutting off their water supply. The Ammonite leader, Achior, explains to Holofernes that the Jews will be protected by their God unless they sin (Jdt 1-7). Judith is introduced only in chapter 8. She chides the leaders of Bethulia for pondering surrender and promises that Yahweh will save the nation through her. By a clever ruse, she enters the enemy camp and beheads Holofernes. She is praised as the savior of the nation (13-16).

Esther. This is a story of the Jewish Diaspora, set in Persia during the reign of Ahasuerus (or Xerxes I: 486-465 B.C.). Esther may center around a historical nucleus, but the present book is most likely a work of didactic fiction describing the divine protection of God's people in a foreign land and explaining the origin of the spring festival of Purim (when the book is read in the Jewish liturgy—9:24-32). The book exists in two forms, a Hebrew edition and a longer Greek edition. The additional material is not simply added at the end of the book but embellishes the Hebrew text at various points (before 1:1 and after 3:12; 4:8; 4:17; 8:12; and 10:3). Interestingly, the Hebrew text makes no mention of God. Jews and Protestants consider only this Hebrew section canonical, but Catholics accept the whole book, including the Greek parts, as biblical. This complexity creates difficulty for tracing citations of the text. The New American Bible uses a system of letter-headings to indicate the Greek sections; the New Jerusalem Bible uses italics.

Esther, a beautiful Hebrew maiden, is chosen to replace Vashti as the queen of Persia. Esther's uncle, Mordecai, a faithful Jew serving at the court, reveals to the king through her a plot of royal assassination. Instead of receiving royal favor, however, Mordecai becomes the object of the rage of Haman, the powerful vizier, for refusing to do homage contrary to Jewish law; and a decree is issued for the slaughter of all Jews in the kingdom. Esther takes the risk of appealing to the king on behalf of her people (6-8). Ahasuerus orders Haman hanged, appoints Mordecai vizier, and approves Jewish self-defense against their enemies (which the Jews carry to extremes). The triumph of the Jews is celebrated with a great feast (9).

The Books of Maccabees. First and Second Maccabees are deuterocanonical books in the Catholic Bible. Unlike other groupings of books (for example, 1 and 2 Kings, 1 and 2 Chronicles), these two works were not written by the same author or group. They deal with the same general period and subject, but from different points of view. First Maccabees is actually the later of the two, written originally in Hebrew around 100 B.C. Second Maccabees was written in Greek in Egypt about 120 B.C.

1 Maccabees. The dating of ancient books usually involves speculation or educated guessing. But there is considerable certainty in the dating of 1 Maccabees to close to 100 B.C. The praise of the Romans in chapter 8 could not have been written by a Palestinian Jew after the takeover by Pompey in 63 B.C. The final verses of the book (16:23-24) speak of the reign of John Hyrcanus, who died in 104 B.C., as past history. The writing must have taken place close to this date because the author seems to use material gathered from eyewitnesses of the Maccabean Revolt (167-164 B.C.). The book also refers to written documents, particularly letters between Jewish and Syrian leaders (such as 10:18-20 and 25-45). First Maccabees contains important historical information for the period 175-134 B.C.

The author viewed the encroachment of pagan Hellenism as a critical challenge to Judaism. God had chosen the Jews for a special covenant relationship; it was essential for them to remain true to the Mosaic Law and to preserve authentic worship. The great enemies of God were not the gentile politicians, who only acted according to their limited understanding, but the apostate Jews who abused their privileged relationship with God. First Maccabees ascribes to God so much holiness and transcendence that God's name is not mentioned at all; God is referred to by imprecise or remote terms like "him" (2:61) or "heaven" (3:18, 50).

The book begins with a quick survey of recent history from the victory of Alexander the Great (333 B.C.) to the accession of Antiochus IV Epiphanes (175 B.C.) and his assaults on Jewish religion in profaning the Temple and prohibiting obedience to the Law (169-167 B.C.). Mattathias leads the revolt against this oppression and at his death appoints his son Judas Maccabeus to take his place (2). Judas wages successful campaigns against the oppressors and against hostile neighbors, purifies the Temple, and makes a treaty with the Romans before his death in 160 B.C. (3-9:22). The remaining chapters describe the careers of Jonathan (9:23-12:54) and Simon (13-16) until the year 134 B.C., ending with a brief reference to the reign of John Hyrcanus.

2 Maccabees. This book is not a sequel to 1 Maccabees. It was written by an Alexandrian Jew several years earlier than 1 Maccabees during the time of John Hyrcanus. First Maccabees covers the period from Antiochus IV's accession to the end of Simon's life (175-134 B.C.); Second Maccabees begins during the time of Seleucus IV (187-175 B.C.) with the treachery of a certain priest named Simon and ends just before the death of Judas Maccabeus in 160 B.C. Literary purpose differs in the two books. First Maccabees recounts the events of recent history as instructive lessons for the readers; Second Maccabees records the historical events to illustrate God's activity. The latter volume attributes Jewish victories to timely interventions from heaven (3:22-34; 10:29-32) and tends to be preachy and moralizing. The author does incorporate documents, however, and provides some historical information for the period not given in 1 Maccabees.

The story proper begins in chapter 3. It is preceded by three addenda. First there is a letter from the Jews in Jerusalem to those in Egypt urging celebration of the feast commemorating the dedication of the Temple (1:10). This letter was written in 124 B.C. and is the latest addition to the book. Following it is a letter dated 164 B.C. announcing the same feast at the time of its inauguration (1:10-2:18). The third addendum is the author's preface (2:19-32) which along with his epilogue (15:37-39) give a rare glimpse of an ancient author's personality. He presents his work as a digest of the five-volume history of Jason of Cyrene (otherwise unknown).

Chapter 3 begins with events leading up to the Maccabean revolt. The high priest Onias defends the Temple treasury from assault with the help of divine warriors (3), but the corruption of subsequent high priests leads to the profanation of the Temple and abolition of the Mosaic Law by Antiochus IV (4-6). Faithful Jews suffer martyrdom rather than violate their faith (6:18-7:42). Judas Maccabeus defends Jewish liberty and purifies the Temple (8-10), and continues to fight successful battles with God's help, climaxing in the defeat of the hated Nicanor (11-15). This book is an important witness to Jewish belief in the resurrection of the just (7:9-14), prayer for the dead (12:39-46), and the intercession of the saints (15:12-16).

Wisdom Literature

All the biblical writings are, as would be expected, affected by the literary forms and conventions current in the world of the writers. None, however, reflect these influences more than the wisdom literature. A widespread wisdom movement reached across national boundaries in the ancient Near East. Wisdom was seen fundamentally as skill in living. Professional court scribes collected the maxims that encapsulated insights distilled from experience. These pearls of wisdom were shared among the cultures. Israel was influenced especially by the wisdom sayings of Egypt and Mesopotamia. The Old Testament writers adapted these materials in key places for the presentation of Yahwistic faith, but otherwise accepted the traditional lore.

Most of the biblical books grouped as wisdom literature

clearly belong to this tradition as it was understood in the contemporary world. The Song of Songs is in an independent category and may have been included only because of its attribution to Solomon. The Psalms incorporate wisdom poetry, but also poems belonging to several other literary categories.

Job. Job has remote forerunners in the literature of Egypt and Mesopotamia but is an original work of genius. It confronts the critical issue of good and evil and their proper rewards. The author presents the conventional wisdom only to challenge it and show its inadequacy for the realities of life. The standard approach (reflected in the Bible in the theology of the Deuteronomist, Psalm 37, some maxims in Proverbs, and elsewhere) is that a good person will be rewarded with health, material prosperity, and general good fortune, while the wicked will suffer the loss of these things.

The author knew that the wicked sometimes prosper and the good sometimes suffer. But conventional wisdom failed to deal with this reality. There could be no appeal to the afterlife at this time in Israel's history (seventh to fifth centuries B.C.). So the author created a story which intensified the conflict of conventional wisdom with real life: a good man, Job, suffers terrible tragedies; his well-meaning friends spin monologue after monologue to prove that Job is secretly evil and must repent. The Book of Job does not profess belief in the resurrection of the just, as is sometimes supposed, but its relentless assault on the accepted doctrine of retribution helped pave the way for belief in life after death.

Readers have always noted how different the beginning and end of the book are from its middle. The traditional "patient Job" is recognizable only in the prologue and epilogue; in the long poetic exchanges, which make up most of the book, Job is impatient and questioning. The author used an existing story expressing the conventional wisdom to serve as the frame for the debate on justice and retribution. Job, a wealthy and good man, is tested by Satan with God's approval. He loses everything but remains faithful to God who has the right to give and take away (1:21); as a reward he receives even more than he had before (42:7-17).

In chapters 3 to 31, Job is visited by his three friends, Eliphaz, Bildad, and Zophar, who try to help him see his plight in the right (wisdom) perspective. He responds to each of their speeches. Chapters 32 to 37 contain the four speeches of Elihu which were probably added to the book by a later writer. The Book of Job reaches its climax in Job 38 to 39; 40:1-5; and 42:1-6, which include the speeches of God and Job's response.

Psalms. The Book of Psalms was compiled in the postexilic period, but many of the religious hymns came from the monarchical and exilic times. About half the psalms are attributed to King David, though he may have had little directly to do with their composition. The group of 150 psalms is internally arranged in five "books" in imitation of the Pentateuch: 1 to 41, 42 to 72, 73 to 89, 90 to 106, and 107 to 150. Each of these sections ends with a doxology, or expression of praise; Psalm 150 is a doxology for the whole Psalter.

The psalms are prayers composed for either individual or group use. Many of them were first used in a liturgical setting. They are Hebrew poetry, employing the techniques of parallelism of lines, imagery, and internal rhythm according to the accents of the individual verse lines. The psalms fall into various literary categories. Some psalms teach wisdom, but many more are laments (personal or community) and hymns of praise. Some of the royal psalms are messianic.

All but thirty-four of the psalms have titles or musical directions appended to them. These were added long after the composition of the psalms. The titles often link the psalm to events of David's life; Psalm 51, for instance, is identified as "A psalm of David, when Nathan the prophet came to him after his affair with Bathsheba." Psalm 51 is also one of the seven penitential psalms (also 6, 32, 38, 102, 130, 143).

References to the psalms have been difficult because of the different systems of enumeration in the Hebrew and Greek (and Latin) texts. This problem is fading now because modern translations accept the Hebrew numbering almost universally; but in the past, Catholic versions were based on the Latin Vulgate and used the Greek numbering which is still cited in older religious books and biblical commentaries. The numbers shift occurs at Psalm 9 (the Greek links Psalms 9 and 10 of the Hebrew together) and affects all the psalms till 147. The following chart shows the correspondences:

Hebrew	Greek/Latin
1-8	1-8
9-10	9
11-113	10-112
114-115	113
116	114-115
117-146	116-145
147	146-147
148-150	148-150

The psalms still contain versification differences because some versions treat the psalm titles as verse 1 of the psalm (NAB), while others start versification with the first words of the psalm (NJB).

Proverbs. The Book of Proverbs was produced by a postexilic writer as a collection of the best of the Israelite wisdom tradition. Some of the material dates back to King Solomon. Parts come from unknown times and sources. Much of it is completely secular. To give a faith context for the collection and to adapt the traditional wisdom to the new needs of his own times, the compiler added an original section of his own to introduce the book (1-9). His keynote is "The fear of the Lord is the beginning of wisdom" (see 1:7; 9:10). He personifies wisdom as the firstborn of God (8:22).

The introductory section is followed by "The Proverbs of Solomon," rules for practical conduct which make up the oldest collection in the book (10:1-22:16) compiled during the reign of Solomon (961-922 B.C.). Two collections of "Sayings of the Wise" (22:17-24:34), dated generally to the preexilic period, show parallels with the Egyptian "Wisdom of Amenemope." The heading of the second collection of the Proverbs of Solomon (25-29) states that "the men of Hezekiah, king of Judah, transmitted them" (25:1), which dates this compilation to about 700 B.C. The book closes with proverbs from two unknown sages, Agur, son of Jakeh the Massaite (30), and Lemuel, king of Massa (31). The latter's contribution is notable in that it is identified as wisdom from his mother rather than his father; and it contains the famous description of the ideal wife.

Ecclesiastes. The title of this book is the Greek translation of the Hebrew name, Qoheleth. It is a symbolic name, "one who calls an assembly." The further identification, "David's son, king of Jerusalem," is meant to evoke the memory of Solomon, though the present work originated in the third century B.C. Ecclesiastes is often compared to the earlier Book of Job because both deal with the question of retribution, finding the standard solutions of the wisdom tradition inadequate to the realities of good and evil in the world.

Ecclesiastes presents the more pessimistic picture of the two. His theme is the vanity of all things. This theme has challenged all interpreters since the early rabbis. How do we reconcile such a negative attitude with faith? The best answer seems to lie in the radical honesty of this believing Israelite who confronts the mystery of life. The wisdom solution of reward or retribution in exchange for good or evil sounded naive, and yet Israel did not have a doctrine of the afterlife. The author does not deny that there is a divine plan to encompass the mystery, but he does deny that facile solutions are a service to God or anyone else. People, even God's people, cannot find enduring happiness by their own resources. Ecclesiastes never offers a definite solution. When a solution comes it will be, like everything else, "given" and not coerced from a sovereign God (3:13-14; 8:15-17).

A later editor, uneasy with the unyielding doctrine of Qoheleth, added a statement about the need for faithful observance of the Law because of God's just retribution (12:13-14). This book is assigned for reading in the Jewish liturgy on the Feast of Tabernacles.

The Song of Songs. The title is a Hebrew way of saying "The greatest of songs." Song of Songs is attributed to Solomon (and called The Song of Solomon in older Protestant versions) though it was produced in the postexilic period. It is a collection of love songs, some of them quite old. The erotic imagery of the poems caused interpreters through the centuries to look for a symbolic meaning; Jewish commentators read the book as a dialogue between Yahweh and Israel (in light of the prophetic tradition which compared Yahweh to the husband and Israel to his bride), and Christians developed this interpretation in terms of Christ and the church.

Modern interpreters are more inclined to see in the Song of Songs a collection of love poems extolling the beauties of human love. As a central gift of God to his people, this human reality is a revelation of God's goodness and an image of his love for his people and all of his creation. Thus the book can be seen as a celebration of the sexual love relationship between a man and a woman, which in turn is a sacramental sign of God's love. This book is read in the Jewish liturgy on the Feast of Passover.

Wisdom. The complete title of this Greek deuterocanonical book is "Wisdom of Solomon." Dated to the middle of the first century B.C., it was the last book of the Old Testament to be written. The author was a Jew of Alexandria in Egypt. He writes in Greek and shows some influences of Hellenistic thought, but has a profound understanding of the Hebrew Scriptures.

The author writes to build up the faith of his fellow Diaspora Jews. The ancient beliefs were severely challenged by new philosophies and scientific discoveries. Some Jews abandoned the faith for paganism. But the answer to the mysteries of life is found in true wisdom, which means faithful adherence to the traditions and practices of Judaism. A long section traces the history of God's saving action in the Exodus, contrasting the protection of the Israelites and the punishment of the Egyptians. Idolatry is presented as the ultimate folly.

The Book of Wisdom addresses the issue of retribution, which also appeared in Job and Ecclesiastes, and makes an important breakthrough toward its solution. There exists a life after death, where the good will be rewarded and the wicked punished (3:1-12). The concept of immortality is expressed clearly (2:23), but there is no mention of a bodily resurrection.

Sirach. The Book of Sirach shares many similarities with the Book of Proverbs. It may be viewed as an updated book of wise instruction for a later situation in Israel. The book was written by "Jesus, son of Eleazar, son of Sirach" (50:27) about the year 180 B.C., during the growing challenge of Hellenism, to convince his fellow Jews that true wisdom lay in the religious traditions of Israel. Sirach was written in Hebrew but until the late 1800s was known to us only through the Greek translation made by the author's grandson after 132 B.C. The translator's preface gives an interesting insight into biblical writing and translation; though it is not canonical, it is included as an introduction to the book in most Bibles.

The author is imbued with love for the Law, the Temple, and the priesthood. He collects maxims dealing with religious and family duties, and covering everyday issues like friendship, the use of wealth, honesty, social conduct, sin, and virtue. These issues, along with praises of wisdom, are contained in the first forty-three chapters, without any discernible overall outline. Chapters 44 to 50 contain a litany of praise for Jewish ancestors from Enoch, Abraham, and the patriarchs to the high priest

Simon, son of Onias (220-195 B.C.). Sirach takes a very low view of the kings of the nation, not mentioning the rulers of Israel and saying of the kings of Judah that "except for David, Hezekiah, and Josiah, they all were wicked" (49:4). The book ends with a hymn of thanksgiving for past favors and an encouragement to readers to seek instruction in wisdom as divine food (51:24).

EIGHT

The New Testament

The formation of the New Testament took place (with the exception of 2 Peter) between A.D. 50 and 100. This process is described in chapter 3. The gospel was revealed in the words and deeds of Jesus and, after his death and resurrection, was preached by his followers with little concern about writing. But there were written collections of Jesus' sayings and some written prayers and hymns for authors to draw from when the first of our New Testament documents began to appear beginning with the writings of Paul in the 50s. Christian self-consciousness was spurred on by the fall of Jerusalem in 70 and by the subsequent hostility between synagogue and Church. The Gospels and some of the other books written after 70 reflect this attitude.

But the concept of a collection of Christian Scriptures on a par with the Hebrew Scriptures emerged only in the second century. Marcion, about A.D. 150, was a major force in establishing the idea of a New Testament, but our first reference to this title comes from Tertullian about 200. It was not till the fourth century that a New Testament canon became fixed. Further information on these developments is available in chapter 3. The present chapter will give more details about the particular books.

Gospels

Mark the evangelist has been credited with creating the literary form we call "gospel." It is not the same as a biography, nor is it a fanciful tale about Jesus (a point Mark's apocryphal imitators did not understand). The idea of a gospel is well stated by John: "Now Jesus did many other signs in the presence of his disciples that are not written in this book. But these are written that you may come to believe that Jesus is the Messiah, the Son of God, and that through this belief you may have life in his name" (Jn 20:30-31). The purpose is not to provide a complete history of Jesus' life, but to increase in the disciples the knowledge of Jesus that will lead to deeper faith and richer life.

Catholic interpretation of the Gospels after Vatican Council II is guided especially by the "Instruction on the Historical Truth of the Gospels" issued by the Pontifical Biblical Commission in 1964. The instruction directs the gospel interpreter to be attentive to three stages in the transmission of the material contained in the sacred texts. The first stage is the time of Jesus' life, roughly the first third of the first century and more precisely the years of his ministry. The second stage includes the period from Jesus' death and resurrection until the writing of the first of our four Gospels (A.D. 30-70). During this time the apostles and other preachers were using the stories about Jesus and applying his words to the lives of their listeners. They were gradually formulating the best methods for teaching his life and message, learning from one another which deeds and sayings to use with particular audiences. The third stage is the time of the writing of the Gospels. The evangelists gathered the wide-ranging material about Jesus, selecting and arranging it in accord with their own purposes. As the Instruction puts it: "From the many things handed down the evangelists selected some things, reduced others to a synthesis, and explained other things according to the needs of the churches.... The truth of the story is not at all affected by the fact that the evangelists relate the words and deeds of the Lord in a different order and express his sayings not literally but differently, while preserving their sense" (paragraph 9).

An awareness of these three stages of development is an invaluable tool for the reader of the Gospels. Divergences in the use or presentation of the sayings and stories from Gospel to Gospel are not causes for alarm. Jesus differed from the other Jewish rabbis in his manner of instructing disciples. He did not emphasize verbatim repetition of his teachings but a personal understanding of himself and his mission. With that, his followers were free to adapt his words to different times without losing the fundamental truth of his message. The evangelists, like the preachers before them, found different ways to present the traditional Gospel material, and the fruit of their reflection has given richer flavor to the message that has come down to us. See, for example, the different uses of a saying like the salt parable (Mt 5:13; Mk 9:50; Lk 14:34-35) or of a story like the cleansing of the Temple (Mt 21:12-17; Mk 11:15-17; Lk 19:45-46; Jn 2:14-16).

With the exception of the Gospels, the description of the individual New Testament books will follow the order in which they appear in the Bible. This is ordinarily easier for reference purposes than a chronological order. But the transposition of Matthew and Mark is more helpful for understanding the originality of Mark and the use of his work by Matthew and Luke.

The first three Gospels are known as the synoptics (from the Greek "to see together") because they follow a common outline. A significant minority of scholars defend the priority of Matthew, but here the widely accepted view that Mark is the first of our gospels will be followed.

Mark. By the time the first of the Gospels appeared, many of the great apostolic leaders (Peter, Paul, James the son of Zebedee, and James of Jerusalem) had already been martyred. The traditional view, still accepted today, is that Mark wrote in Rome for gentile Christians. The time of writing, scholars suppose, was between A.D. 65 and 75, depending on whether it preceded or followed the destruction of Jerusalem.

Mark wrote an action Gospel. He describes Jesus' preaching and teaching ministry but preserves very few of his actual words. For this reason the Gospel of Mark was overshadowed for centuries by the Gospels of Matthew and Luke, which contain both Jesus' actions and teachings. When Mark was "rediscovered" by scholars in the nineteenth century, his work was considered important by them because of its untouched, primitive quality— not dressed up or expanded by the evangelist's own reflections.

This view did an injustice to the evangelist. Like an artist, Mark carefully selected and arranged the episodes he included in his Gospel. His major concern was to focus attention squarely on the person of Jesus. The opening verse is his title and statement of purpose: "The beginning of the gospel of Jesus Christ, the Son of God" (1:1). A formal recognition of Jesus as the Messiah (Christ) by his contemporaries comes at the middle of the book (8:29), and his divine sonship is proclaimed at the end (15:39). Jesus is not the kind of Messiah his contemporaries had been expecting. He is not a warrior-king like David; and the political independence of Judea is not on his agenda. He is a suffering Messiah on the model of the Servant of Yahweh described by Isaiah.

Even Jesus' closest followers were not able to understand this kind of Messiah. Peter, their spokesman, is called Satan because of his failure to recognize this point (8:32-33). Jesus tried to keep his messianic identity secret (1:44; 5:43) until he would have a chance to explain its true meaning while on the journey to Jerusalem. Three predictions of his fate in Jerusalem punctuate these chapters (8:31; 9:31; 10:32-34). The fulfillment comes in the Passion account, which in Mark is stark and unsoftened (14-15). But the last word is victory, the Resurrection (16).

The original manuscript of Mark ended at 16:8. From the earliest times this ending seemed too abrupt to some readers. An alternate ending, 16:9-20, was formulated with the help of information from the other Gospels. This section, though not written by Mark, is considered canonical and inspired. Two other endings appear in later manuscripts and are printed in some Bibles.

Matthew. The Gospels of Matthew and Luke were written at approximately the same time, around A.D. 85, but with very different audiences and purposes. Matthew wrote mainly for a Jewish Christian community, probably in Syria; Luke for a Greek Christian community in Asia Minor. Both used the Gospel of Mark as their general outline. They also included a separate collection of Jesus' stories (with many sayings) referred to by scholars as Q (from the German word *Quelle*, "source") in addition to independent information of their own.

Matthew also has similarities with John's Gospel, not in outline or method, but in ecclesiastical context. Both appear to have been written during the period of intense hostility between Jews and Christians which existed after the fall of Jerusalem and the destruction of the Temple. Until that catastrophic event, Jewish Christians felt free to maintain their Jewish practices and relationships. But in order to protect the fragile unity of Judaism after A.D. 70, the rabbis excommunicated all except the followers of the pure Mosaic Law. This split families and caused other bitter repercussions. The resulting hostility is reflected in Matthew and John.

Matthew incorporated 600 of Mark's 661 verses but added an equal amount of additional material, much of it the teaching of Jesus. He is concerned to demonstrate that Jesus is the Messiah promised from of old and that everything that has happened to and through him is the fulfillment of the Old Testament. This is a main theme of his infancy narrative, which begins with a genealogy stressing the continuity of Abraham, David, and Jesus, and which is based on five "formula quotations" showing the fulfillment of the Old Testament.

Some scholars support the notion that Matthew left a self-portrait in his description of a Christian scribe: "Every scribe who has been instructed in the kingdom of heaven is like the head of a household who brings from his storeroom both the new and the old" (13:52). Matthew evidently possessed great abilities of organization and synthesis. His Gospel bears the imprint of a careful architect. In between the infancy narrative (1-2) and the passion account (26-28), the author has arranged Jesus' words and deeds into five large sections, each containing an action narrative and a teaching: 3-7; 8-11:1; 11:2-13:53; 13:54-19:1; 19:2-26:1. Notable among the discourses are the Sermon on the Mount (5-7) and the advice to a divided community (17:22-19:1). The latter is a good example of the application of Jesus' teaching to current needs of the Church in a later time.

Luke. About the same time that Matthew was composing his Gospel with converts from Judaism in mind, Luke was putting the message into a form understandable and acceptable to educated Greek converts from paganism. Luke is the most polished and urbane of the evangelists, probably a native of Asia Minor and a graduate of the imperial schools. He was trained in the conventions of contemporary Greek historiography and used his skill to convince his readers that Christianity was a religion to be taken seriously by the educated citizen.

But Luke was also well-versed in the Septuagint, the Greek version of the Old Testament, with its Hebrew thought patterns and rhythms of speech. He was able to use different modes of discourse in his Gospel: a classical Greek literary pattern for his introduction (1:1-4), Hebrew-flavored Greek for his infancy narrative (1:5-2:52), and a normal style for the balance of his work. This careful control extends at times even to the words that he reserves for particular stages of his narrative.

The Gospel of Luke is the first part of a two-part work. This evangelist is the only one of the four to have written a sequel to his Gospel. His Acts of the Apostles carries the story of Jesus into the early years of the Church. He probably intended that the two parts would remain together in publication, but since the time of the early Church they have been separated by the Gospel of John.

Luke's readers, scattered throughout the Roman empire far from Palestine late in the first century, were in danger of losing contact with their roots. The evangelist shows the steady unfolding of the plan of salvation under the direct guidance of

God. It began in a remote corner of a small country, but through witnesses divinely chosen, the Good News spread to the whole Mediterranean world. Some of the Christian heroes of the first generation were only recently dead and others were still carrying God's word to those who would accept it.

Luke's infancy narrative, like Matthew's, shows the coming of Jesus as the fulfillment of Jewish hopes. But his method is quite different. Luke reveals the fulfillment by subtle allusion rather than by formula quotations. Jesus is paralleled with John the Baptist but shown to be much superior. After the baptism and Galilee ministry, Luke supplements traditional material with information from his own sources to form an expanded narrative of Jesus' final journey to Jerusalem (9:51-19:44). In this section we meet some of the most-loved portions of Luke's Gospel: the Good Samaritan, Martha and Mary, the Prodigal Son, the Rich Man and Lazarus, the Pharisee and the Tax Collector, and Zaccheus.

Luke presents Jesus as the Savior, highlighting his compassion toward the poor, the outcast, the oppressed. He shows Jesus' harshness toward those who misuse their wealth and power, but also his openness toward those who know how to use these privileges for the good of all. Jesus possesses a special sensitivity to the gifts and the needs of women. In fact, he is open to everyone, and the salvation he brings is meant not only for the Jews but for all the world.

John. It was mentioned above that the Gospel of John shares with Matthew a context of hostility between Jews and Christians after the fall of Jerusalem. John's Gospel is usually dated about a decade later than Matthew's, sometime in the 90s. The division is very sharp in John, so much so that Jesus' enemies are simply called "the Jews" and are identified as children of the devil (8:44). Recent commentators have also discerned in this Gospel evidence of various divisions among Christians during the evangelist's time.

John's positive purpose in writing the Gospel, however, was to strengthen faith in Jesus through knowledge of his "signs" (20:30-31), and that message should be the focus of the reader's attention. "Sign" is an important word in Johannine theology. The miracles of Jesus are not called "acts of power" as in the synoptics, but "signs." Jesus himself is the Great Sign of God in the world; he is the revelation of the Father (1:18). John emphasizes Jesus' divinity and shows him in constant command of the various situations, including the Passion.

But John is different from the synoptics in other ways as well. Seven signs are the only miracles he mentions, and only three of these are recorded in the synoptics. Jesus makes only one trip to Jerusalem in the synoptics, but several in John; it is from John that we get the idea of a three-year instead of a one-year ministry. Jesus dies a day earlier in John. Various figures in John's Gospel take on a symbolic significance beyond their historical identity, such as Nicodemus, the Samaritan woman, the man born blind. Mary is never named but called the "mother of Jesus" or "woman" (2:1-12; 19:25-26). A mysterious figure often identified as John the apostle is "the disciple whom Jesus loved" (21:7; see also 13:23; 19:26), the ideal follower of Jesus.

John's emphasis on Jesus' divinity begins with the opening verses of his Gospel. The traditional early preaching, as exemplified in the outline of Mark's Gospel, had begun with the baptism in the Jordan; Matthew and Luke took the story back to the infancy; John, the latest to write, introduced the Savior as the preexisting Word of God. In the long discourses of his

Gospel, Jesus calls on his Father to bear witness to the unique relationship between them; the Father has given him everything and made him the source of salvation (6:38-40). In a major confrontation with "the Jews," Jesus attributes to himself the title "I AM" reserved for God (8:24, 28, 58; see Ex 3:14). Still, Jesus is human, the Word made flesh, and suffers real death at the hands of his enemies (19:30-35). This death is not the end, but the beginning of the spread of salvation through the gift of the Spirit (19:30; 20:22-23).

Acts of the Apostles. The sequel to Luke's Gospel begins, as his first book did, with a formal dedication to Theophilus, probably an influential convert in Asia Minor. The Greek title of the work is given as "Acts of Apostles," not a complete summary but a record of the careers of some of the most important apostles in the initial development of the Church and its mission to the world. Luke consciously parallels Acts with the Gospel, beginning with a "birth" through the overshadowing of the Spirit (2), describing preaching and miracle-working (3: 1-5:16), and a martyr's death like that of Jesus (7:59-60). The second half of the book parallels Paul with Jesus.

The issue dominating the first chapters is the question of membership in the fellowship of Jesus. Is it reserved for Jews or may pagans be baptized? What about circumcision and the other observances of the Law of Moses? Jesus and his first disciples were all Jews, so this was a new question without a precedent to follow. Gradually, the Spirit given at Pentecost guides the community to a decision: through the baptism of Samaritans and an Ethiopian convert to Judaism (8) and eventually even the baptism of pagans (10-11). The matter is formally decided by the leaders at the Council of Jerusalem (15); after this the book becomes a travelogue detailing Paul's missionary journeys and his voyage to Rome.

Geography is theological in the writings of Luke. Jesus moves from a remote village in Galilee to Jerusalem, the heart of Judaism, where salvation is achieved through his death and Resurrection. The church is formed in Jerusalem by the power of the Spirit; then the word of God is carried to Judea and Samaria, to Antioch, to Asia Minor, and finally to the center of the empire, Rome, from which the gospel will be disseminated to "the ends of the earth" (1:8).

In writing his Gospel for imperial citizens, Luke stresses that there is nothing unpatriotic about Christianity. Paul points to his Roman citizenship several times (22:25-28); his arrests are always on false charges or else on religious matters on which Roman law has no bearing (18:14-15). Paul takes every opportunity to preach the gospel to Romans (24:24-26), and at the end of the book is under house arrest in Rome preaching about Jesus "with complete assurance and without hindrance" (28:31).

The Letters of Paul

The second major section of the New Testament, after the narratives about Jesus and the foundation of the Church, belongs to the writings of Paul. The New Testament contains thirteen letters, or epistles, under his name besides the Letter to the Hebrews, which is often associated with him. The impact of his teaching on the Christian Church through the centuries is inestimable.

Romans. St. Paul wrote this letter to Rome from Corinth in A.D. 57 while he was on his third missionary journey. Paul addressed most of his epistles to communities he had founded, conveying messages of correction or encouragement. But Paul's letter to the Romans is in some ways his self-introduction to a community he had never visited. The apostle knew that various reports of his teaching had reached Rome; he wanted to present his position on some things clearly in case there had been misrepresentation. He also took the opportunity, in preparation for his visit, to comment on some issues debated in the Roman community.

By the time Paul wrote, there was a sizable Christian community in Rome. It had been founded by converts from Judaism, but the majority of the community were gentile Christians. Paul said a lot about the relationship of Christianity to Judaism. First of all, he insisted strongly that salvation comes by faith and not by observances, not even by observance of the sacred Law of Moses. He minced no words when treating this topic earlier in his Letter to the Galatians. Here he says the same things but from a calmer and broader perspective.

Paul identifies himself in chapter 1 and states his theme in concise terms (1:16-17). He proceeds to demonstrate that no one can gain righteousness without the help of God (1:18-3:20). Salvation comes through faith in Jesus Christ (3:21-5:21). The Christian life brings a threefold liberation: from sin and death, from self, and from the Law (6-7). This first part of the letter reaches its climax in chapter 8, a description of the gift of the Spirit that makes it possible for human beings to achieve the destiny planned by God.

Chapters 9 to 11 treat the question of the meaning of God's covenant with the Jews now that a new covenant has been ratified in Jesus. A section on the moral duties of Christians follows (12:1-15:13), then the conclusion (15:14-16:27). Scholars still debate about the authenticity of chapter 16, because it does not appear in some of the ancient manuscripts. Some think that the list may have become separated from another letter, but the common view is to regard the chapter as part of Romans.

1 Corinthians. Paul wrote this letter toward the end of his long stay in Ephesus in the spring of A.D. 57. He had founded the Christian community of Corinth in 50 or 51 and tried to keep in touch with the stormy developments there. This letter was written in answer to a number of questions brought to him by representatives from Corinth. The city, serving as a port to two seas, was notorious for its moral depravity. Besides coping with this, the Corinthian Christians were confronted with all the questions raised by the Hellenistic patterns of the empire.

The apostle begins immediately to attack the divisions that have emerged in the Corinthian community (1-4). The believers claim various leaders as the founders of their factions; some claim a superior wisdom which would put them on a higher spiritual level. Paul states that the only true wisdom is the folly of the cross, and that the very leaders they are claiming as their patrons are "fools on Christ's account" (4:10).

Before dealing with the questions addressed to him, Paul discusses other problems of which he is aware. He addresses cases of incest and other sexual immorality and chides members of the community for taking their private quarrels into the arena of public law (5-6). The answers to particular questions beginning in chapter 7 have greatly influenced the history of Christianity: marriage and virginity (7), charity in religious observance (8-9), the Eucharist and other assemblies for worship (10-11), spiritual gifts (12-14), the resurrection of the body (15). In speaking of the gifts of the Spirit, Paul uses the analogy of the body for the first time in describing the unity of believers with Christ (12:12-31) and pens the famous hymn to love (13).

2 Corinthians. Paul wrote this letter from Ephesus also probably a few months after 1 Corinthians. In the early chapters, Paul expresses personal affection for the readers and his deep love of the gospel. In the closing pages he makes a sharp defense of his apostleship. The striking differences among the sections of this letter, particularly between chapters 1 to 9 and 10 to 13, have prompted various theories of composition. The majority opinion today is that the letter is from Paul, but that it did not originally exist as a unified document. Paul refers to other letters to the Corinthians which we no longer have (1 Cor 5:9; 2 Cor 2:4). Perhaps the jarring material in 2 Corinthians has been added from those documents.

Sometime after he wrote 1 Corinthians, Paul heard that he was being criticized at Corinth and that his apostleship had even been called into question. The Corinthians' attitude hurt Paul deeply. In his second letter, the apostle describes his trials for the gospel and tries to convince the Corinthians of his sincerity. Paul describes his apostolic work as a "ministry of reconciliation" (5:18) in which the gospel is carried to the world like a treasure contained in earthen vessels (4:7). In chapters 8 and 9 Paul encourages generosity in a collection for the community in Jerusalem.

Paul's defense of his ministry becomes much more aggressive in chapters 10 to 13. He is scornful of adversaries who "recommend themselves" (10:12) and those who are "false apostles" (11:13). Paul paints a vivid history of his own labors and sufferings for the gospel (11-12); he reproaches himself for letting himself be driven to such foolishness by the criticisms of those he has served. In the closing chapter he issues a final challenge to his opponents, warning them to prepare for his arrival.

Galatians. The dating of this letter fluctuates between A.D. 50 and 55, but the later date, early in Paul's stay at Ephesus, seems more likely, especially because of the similarity of themes and expressions in the subsequent Letter to the Romans (57). Galatia is a region in Asia Minor where Paul founded a community in the early 50s on his second missionary journey. In this letter we meet the apostle at his most exasperated, trying to snuff out a fire he thought had already been well doused. The Galatian community has welcomed Jewish-Christian teachers from Jerusalem who are demanding that the gentile converts observe the Mosaic Law. These "Judaizers" are draining all the meaning from the saving work of Christ.

In Romans, Paul introduces himself as the "slave" of Jesus Christ. Here, leading with his authority, he identifies himself as "an apostle not from human beings nor through a human being but through Jesus Christ and God the Father" (1:1). After a brief introduction he addresses the issue immediately without the customary thanksgiving. Then follows a brief expression of amazement at the Galatians' susceptibility to error, after which Paul returns to the issue of his authority, providing us with our only firsthand account of an apostolic call in the New Testament (1:11-17). Paul reports the decision of the Council of Jerusalem (see Acts 15) but is very concerned to show his independence from the other leaders as a chosen apostle (2:1-14).

In chapter 3 Paul presents his basic argument for justification by faith; this is developed in Romans 3 to 4. Over and over again he stresses the freedom of the Christian, which is undermined by a dependence on legal observances (4). Works have their place in the life of faith only as the overflow of love: "In Christ Jesus, neither circumcision nor uncircumcision counts for anything, but only faith working through love" (5:6). He goes on to explain that he argues not for an undisciplined license but for an interior freedom guided by the Spirit (5:13-26).

Though Paul is harsh in this letter, his love for the Galatians shines through. The vigor of his language is only meant to impress upon the readers his serious concern for their happiness and salvation. The best way to fulfill the true law, the law of Christ, is to "bear one another's burdens" (6:2). He tries to lift a false burden from their shoulders and is willing to suffer their displeasure or the scorn of their teachers if only he may bring them back to the peace, mercy, and grace of Jesus (6:14-18).

Ephesians. As Galatians and Romans are related by theme and terminology, so are Ephesians and Colossians. One major difference is that while there is no doubt that Paul is the author of Galatians and Romans, there is a growing consensus that Ephesians, probably, and Colossians, possibly, were written by later disciples of the Pauline tradition. The style and argument of these letters is quite different from the standard recognizable in the more certain Pauline letters. In the case of Colossians, there is still a strong case for the position that this difference may be explained by a secretary's freedom in turning spoken phrases into a polished written document.

Ephesians is the later production (and has probably used the text of Colossians); it is now often dated vaguely to late in the first century. Its key teaching is on the nature of the Church. The concept of the Church builds on the teaching of Paul, especially the image of the body of Christ, but expands the Pauline notion of the local community as Church to a worldwide or even cosmic vision of the body of Christians with Christ as head. Ephesians stresses the unity of the Church (4:3-6) and its holiness (1:4; 5:25-27). Though Ephesians contains a section of moral instructions (5-6), there is no mention of concrete problems as in the letters to Corinth and Galatia. This vagueness of reference, coupled with the fact that the direction to Ephesus in 1:1 is missing in many manuscripts, has led to the supposition that the document was meant as a general letter for believers rather than as a message for one particular community.

The first chapter presents a vision of God's overall plan of unity in Christ (1). The gratuity of God's gift toward the gentiles in bringing them into a share of the fulfillment of the ancient promises is then stressed (2). The writer explains Paul's mission in the manner of earlier letters (3). The final three chapters call for a life worthy of the Christian calling. Special emphasis is given to household relationships: husbands and wives, children and parents, slaves and masters (5-6).

Philippians. Philippians is grouped with Ephesians, Colossians, and Philemon in the "Captivity Lettters." Paul wrote Philippians from prison possibly in Ephesus sometime before 1 Corinthians, therefore in A.D. 55 or 56. According to Acts 16, he founded the Christian community at Philippi, his first on European soil, during his second missionary journey. The congregation at Philippi greatly respected Paul, and he shows evident affection for them. He encourages them to continue in their faithful following of Jesus and expresses the wish that they will share his own deep joy which is undiminished by the confines of prison. He also warns them against Judaizers, the same group which called forth his intervention in Galatia.

Philippians, like 2 Corinthians, seems to be a composite of more than one letter. Scholars distinguish three different letters or parts of letters to Philippi. They would have been combined by a later editor under a single introduction and conclusion so that the smaller parts would not be lost and in order to save copyists time and materials.

The first and longest section begins with 1:1 and continues to 3:1 with a skip to the conclusion in 4:4-9. Paul speaks of his imprisonment but without concern for the future; he is joyful and confident in the Lord's power to bring good from his suffering. He speaks of the situation at Philippi and, in encouraging love among the members of the Church, incorporates a beautiful hymn on Jesus' self-emptying love (2:5-11). He talks about his plans for serving them through his assistants, Timothy and Epaphroditus (2:19-30), and ends on a note of joy.

The second section (3:2-4:3) responds more directly to the problem of false teachers who have been infiltrating the community. Paul describes his own attitude in following Jesus through suffering to resurrection and offers himself as a model rather than those who are urging adherence to the Law. The third section is very short (4:10-23), a thank-you note for aid the community sent Paul when he was in need in Thessalonica.

Colossians. The relationship of Colossians to Ephesians was mentioned earlier. Both show a late development of Paul's doctrine of the Church as the body of Christ. If Colossians was written by Paul, rather than a later disciple, the best date would be A.D. 61-63, during Paul's confinement in Rome (Acts 28).

The Christian community at Colossae in Asia Minor was founded by Epaphras, a gentile Christian, probably one of

Paul's converts. Epaphras visited Paul in prison and brought news of some problems in the Colossian church caused by superstitious teachings. One doctrine seems to have come from Greek sources: the idea that human affairs are controlled by angelic beings who must be appeased; the other was the familiar Judaizing emphasis on observances of the Mosaic Law. Some of the false teachers were advertising a secret knowledge beyond the gospel, to which Paul responded that perfect knowledge is found in Christ (2:3).

Paul opens with his customary thanksgiving, commending the Colossians for their faith, hope, and love (1:3-4). He repeats this approval later in the epistle (2:5), which indicates that so far the false teachers have made only insignificant inroads. Paul describes the preeminence of Christ with the help of a beautiful liturgical hymn (1:15-20). He then explains his role as minister of the mystery of Christ, and follows with a warning against the false teachers (2:4-23). Christian life is portrayed as a new existence empowered by the resurrection (3). The letter ends with final admonitions and information about the apostle's situation and his plans (4).

1 Thessalonians. First Thessalonians carries special significance because it is the earliest work in the New Testament. Paul founded the community at Thessalonica in northern Greece on his second missionary journey in the year 50. This event aroused severe Jewish hostilities (according to Acts 17:1-10), so much so that Paul and Silas left town by night. Paul went south to Athens for a fruitless attempt at preaching to the philosophers, and then moved on to Corinth. Concerned about the firmness of the foundation in Thessalonica, Paul sent Timothy to give the community support and encouragement (3:2-3). Timothy reported to him at Corinth that the Thessalonians were remaining faithful and progressing well. This was the occasion for Paul's letter to them.

In later letters Paul's thanksgiving will occupy a few of the opening lines. Here his thankfulness and happiness over the good news from Thessalonica continues for two chapters. The apostle impresses on his hearers the importance of their faith for the spread of the gospel elsewhere (1:8; 3:8). An interesting feature of this opening section is Paul's description of his work among them: he wants to distance himself from religious frauds who were using their preaching for personal gain (2:5-9). Paul gives advice to help the Thessalonians continue in their Christian conversion (3:9-4:12).

A particular concern at this early period of the Church was the doctrine of the "Parousia," or second "coming," of Christ. Christians believed that this was going to happen very soon. The Thessalonians were distressed because some of their members had died; they feared these departed believers would not be able to share the joy of the second coming. Paul replies that death will in no way deprive faithful Christians of this victory (4:13-17). In his final words Paul calms the anxieties of these new Christians, telling them that the best preparation for the coming of Christ is the faithful and loving conduct of daily responsibilities (5).

2 Thessalonians. Not long after sending the letter to the Thessalonians, Paul felt the need to write again. His admonitions about the second coming were not heeded. The imminent coming of the Lord still agitated some of the community. Paul was especially concerned about those who stopped working because the end was near. They gave the community a bad reputation just at the time persecution intensified. Because of the more impersonal style of this letter and the different treatment of some issues dealt with in 1 Thessalonians, some scholars believe 2 Thessalonians was written by a later disciple in Paul's name.

Paul's introduction addresses words of comfort to the community in distress from persecution (1:3-10). He then confronts the issue of the Parousia, which had probably become more acute because of suffering. The apostle reassures his readers, reminding them of his earlier teaching that certain events must precede the coming of Jesus (2:1-12). Paul refers to the mysterious "lawless one" who will do Satan's work but be overcome by the Lord. This figure and the reference to "what is restraining" (2:6) elude our understanding today.

Paul emphasized that the important thing is to remain firm without fear, holding fast to the traditional truth (2:13-17). The final chapter evokes Paul's own example of work as a contrast to the Thessalonians who are sitting idle. Paul asks the community to pray for him but reminds them that he, and not the troublesome teachers, speaks with God's authority.

1 Timothy. First and Second Timothy and Titus are grouped together as the "Pastoral Letters." They reflect a Church order of the late first century and are generally acknowledged to have been written by a disciple or group after Paul's death. These letters provide a window to the next stage of development after the Acts of the Apostles. The communities founded by the roving missionaries have special needs for continuing stability. Thus the pastoral letters stress sound doctrine and the rules for choosing leaders.

Acts describes Timothy as the son of a Hebrew mother and

a Greek father (Acts 16:1). He was the companion of Paul on some of his journeys. Here he is stationed in Ephesus as the leader of the local Christian community (1 Tm 1:3). The letters contain Pauline advice for exercising this role. First Timothy begins with an attack on the teachers of false doctrines (1). Then Paul reviews rules for correct conduct in liturgical assemblies (2) and a list of qualifications for various ministries in the community (3). The letter returns to the issue of false doctrine, this time concerned with misguided asceticism (4:1-5). The final two chapters give practical advice for guiding widows, presbyters (elders with some leadership responsibilities), slaves, and their masters.

2 Timothy. This letter is more of a personal message from Paul to Timothy than the first one. In 1 Timothy advice was given for problems in leading a community; here Paul speaks of his own situation, confessing a feeling of loneliness and abandonment, and gives personal encouragement to Timothy, "my dear child" (1:2). But the tone of this letter is more severe in some ways. Some followers have defected from the faith. Timothy must hold to his sacred charge and rely on the just judgment of God to vindicate and reward him after his difficult labors are over.

The personal tone is set immediately with the description of the last meeting of Paul and Timothy and references to the latter's family (1:4-5). The apostle confesses to feeling the pains of desertions (1:15); he tells Timothy what he considers essential for a good Christian leader in these difficult times (2). Paul offers himself as a model for the young Timothy (3:10-17) and repeats the commission of a sacred charge (4:1-5). With "I have competed well" (4:7) and his instructions about his cloak, papyrus rolls, and parchments (4:13), Paul sounds like an old warrior signing off.

Titus. Titus is known to us from the letters of Paul as a Greek convert (Gal 2:1-3) who fulfilled several important missions for the apostle (2 Cor 7:6-7; 8:16-18). Paul called him "my partner and co-worker for you" (2 Cor 8:23). The letter to Titus indicates that Titus was left on the island of Crete to finish Paul's work there. Paul is sending more detailed instruction for this work.

This letter is closer in theme to 1 Timothy than to 2 Timothy. The fluid state of church order is reflected, however, in the fact that though in 1 Timothy the offices of bishop and presbyter were distinct, in Titus they are equated. Chapter 1 gives the qualifications for a Christian leader with the familiar warnings about false teachers; chapter 2 contains practical counsel for family relations; chapter 3 expands this to responsibilities in the broader society.

Philemon. This letter is unique among the writings of Paul, a personal letter on a personal matter. We are fortunate that the early Christians did not lose this jewel. Philemon was a prominent member of the Christian community at Colossae. Paul writes him about his runaway slave, Onesimus (Col 4:9). What he says has a bearing on the institution of slavery, but speaks more to us about the new relationship believers share in Christ. This letter is certainly authentic. Its date depends on the location of Paul's imprisonment, either Rome (A.D. 61-63) or Ephesus (around 55).

Paul adapts his usual letter pattern to this shortest of his extant writings. He greets Philemon and his family, then thanks

God for the good reports he has heard about their Christian influence. The body of the letter is a plea to Philemon's conscience: he cannot behave toward Onesimus, also a Christian, as if neither master nor slave knew Christ. Paul applies a little personal pressure at the end to bolster his argument.

Hebrews. This beautiful document has been known in tradition as "Paul's Letter to the Hebrews," but it was not written by Paul nor is it a letter. Its difference in style and thought from other New Testament writings made its canonicity debatable until late in the fourth century. The idea that Paul was the author probably came from the mention of Timothy in 13:23. But it is evident that this polished Greek sermon comes from a time late in the first century and from an author knowledgeable in Platonic philosophy. Most scholars locate this author in Alexandria, Egypt.

The title "to the Hebrews," added a hundred years later, is also of little help in knowing for whom this document was intended. Arguments support both Jewish and gentile Christian addressees. The identity of the author and original recipients is not important for reading the sermon; it is written to strengthen the faith of believers and to give them a deeper insight into the mystery of Christ.

Hebrews is noted for its balanced emphasis on the divinity and humanity of Jesus. This is evident right from the beginning. Jesus is God's ultimate word, higher than the angels (1), but he abased himself to become human and die for us (2). Because he is one of us, Jesus can understand us when we approach his throne (2:18; 4:15-16). Jesus is the fulfillment of Jewish hopes. He brings the rest that the people of God had been looking for (3-4).

The central section of the book (5-10) presents Jesus as the eternal high priest whose sacrifice overcomes sin once and for all and establishes a new covenant with God. The theology of Christ the priest "according to the order of Melchizedek" is unique in the New Testament (7). The author centers on the saving death of Jesus as the means by which a new access to God has been opened up.

The third major section (11-12) turns to the practical living out of the Christian salvation described earlier. The author presents models of faith from Judaism (reminiscent of the lists of heroes in the books of Sirach and Wisdom) leading to the supreme model, Jesus. Here the author urges members of the Christian Church to forge ahead in faith and hope on pilgrimage to the heavenly Jerusalem (12:22). The sermon closes with exhortations for daily Christian living (13), including the warning about false teaching which is practically standard in Christian literature of the time.

James. The next seven letters in the New Testament have been known traditionally as the "Catholic Epistles" because the ancient interpreters considered them addressed to the whole Church rather than to individuals or communities. The letter of James is addressed to the "twelve tribes in the dispersion," a Jewish designation probably meant as a symbol for the Christian Church scattered throughout the Roman empire. The author is either James, the leader of the Jerusalem community (Acts 12:17) who died in the early sixties, or, as is more likely because of the Hellenistic language and the developed state of the Church, an anonymous disciple from the eighties or nineties.

The book is written in the spirit of the Old Testament wisdom literature and bears comparison with Proverbs and Sirach for its themes (such as wisdom, humility, use of the tongue, public behavior) and for its loose organization. Though the author shows familiarity with earlier New Testament writings, Jesus is mentioned only twice (1:1; 2:1) and reference to concepts specifically Christian is rare. One of these references is to the controversy over faith and works (2:14-26). To Luther this passage seemed (mistakenly) to contradict Paul's teaching on justification in Galatians and Romans; he gave James a secondary status among the New Testament writings, but the book was restored to its traditional place by later Protestants.

Chapters 1 and 4 contain various rules for conduct. Chapter 3 is well known for its graphic imagery on the use of the tongue. Chapter 5 contains one of the few passages that have been officially interpreted by the Catholic Church. The Council of Trent declared that 5:14-15 refers to the Sacrament of Anointing of the Sick.

1 Peter. The addressees of this letter, like those of James, are "dispersed" throughout the world, but in this instance, the world is localized as Asia Minor (1:1). Later in the letter we find out that the readers live under danger of persecution. This is what makes them "sojourners": they are aliens in the pagan world. This letter is dated, therefore, to the 90s, quite likely the work of a Christian pastor writing in the name of Peter. Unlike James, 1 Peter's moral exhortations are closely related to Christian salvation themes. The beautiful baptismal exposition has given rise to the suggestion that some of the materials originated in early baptismal liturgy.

The baptismal theme is introduced with a striking prayer of praise to the Father relating our new birth in Christ to the resurrection (1:3-5). The end of the first chapter (1:18-20) highlights the role of the death of Jesus in salvation. The rest of the book is an instruction on the response to this rich inheritance in living the Gospel. Though Christians are treated as strangers and exiles, they should live as good citizens (2:11-17). An example of early Christian application of the Old Testament is the reflection of Jesus as the Suffering Servant of Isaiah in 2:21-25. First Peter provides particular admonitions for married couples (3), for Church leaders, and for young men (5). Recurring themes for all the believers are mutual charity and fidelity in the midst of suffering.

2 Peter. Second Peter is regarded today as the latest document in the New Testament. It reflects a Church structure similar to that of the Pastorals of Paul and incorporates much of the letter of Jude, which dates to the last part of the first century. Second Peter refers to a collection of Paul's letters (3:15-16); such a collection was not made until the 90s. This author, like the author of 1 Peter, writes in the name of the great apostle to address needs of the Church in a later time: in this case, to discuss the difficulty caused by the delay of the second coming of Jesus (the Parousia). Second Peter is generally dated by scholars early in the second century.

The letter is addressed in a general way to all Christians of the time, a mixture of converts from Judaism and paganism. The author is concerned about the challenge to orthodox teaching, particularly the denial of the Lord's coming and a consequent disregard for proper Christian conduct. Chapter 1 claims the authority of Peter with reference to his unique privilege as a witness of the Transfiguration of Jesus (1:16-18). The punishment of evildoers is proved from past history (2). False teachers are warned, and the true teaching about the coming of the Lord is taught by one who is qualified to interpret the

Scriptures (3).

1 John. We have become familiar by now, after reviewing the preceding several documents, with the practice of attributing late New Testament writings to the great apostles (see also chapter 3). Johannine epistles are another important example. The Gospel of John reflected the situation (around A.D. 90) of the community which had taken its inspiration from the "beloved disciple." This group of Christians probably centered around Ephesus in Asia Minor. The Gospel of John showed the followers of Jesus in bitter struggle with the Jews. First, Second, and Third John point to a situation in the Johannine community about a decade later, therefore at the turn of the century. Here groups of Christians argue over the correct interpretation of the gospel. The author of the Johannine letters, probably not the same as the author of the Gospel, writes against the people he considers false teachers, "antichrists" who "went out from us" (2:18,19). These false teachers have distorted the teaching about Jesus and the Christian life presented in the Gospel of John.

The principal error of the adversaries was the minimizing of Jesus' humanity. First John begins with a dramatic and graphic description of the "Word of life" as something heard, seen, and touched. This theme appears again in 2:18-23 and 4:1-6. A destructive moral teaching flowed from disregard for the human reality of Jesus: the human actions of his followers are not important either. Therefore the admonition to "keep my commandments" (Jn 15:10) is undermined. Those who deny sinfulness, the "liars," are mentioned in 1:6-10 and 4:20-21. The author is especially concerned about disregard for the commandment to love one another and has penned some of the most memorable lines on love in the New Testament (3:11-23; 4:7-21).

2 John. In 2 and 3 John the author introduces himself as "the Presbyter," that is, the "elder," probably a title indicating his prestige and authority as a disciple of the first followers of Jesus. He wrote to "the chosen Lady and to her children," members of a Christian community, to encourage them and warn them against dangers that may be coming. The dangers were those mentioned in 1 John, particularly the overly "progressive" view about Jesus (9) which disregards his humanity, his "coming in the flesh" (7).

3 John. The Johannine author had mentioned an intention to visit the community addressed in 2 John (2 Jn 12). In 3 John he writes to a different group to encourage the acceptance of the missionaries he will send (5-8). The local leader, a certain Diotrephes, was unfriendly to these traveling preachers (9-10). The author intends to visit soon to straighten out the problem. This letter reveals friction between two orders of leadership in the early Church.

Jude. The author identifies himself not as the apostle Jude but as the "brother of James," the leader of the Jerusalem community (Acts 15:13). Jude and James are linked as relatives of Jesus in Mark 6:3 (where his name is sometimes translated "Judas"). Jude's letter seems to date from late in the century, however, because of its reference to "the apostles of our Lord Jesus Christ" (17) as a group from the past. Jude warns about false teachers who are "intruders"(4) in the Church. Their error is more in their sinful practice than in some particular doctrine.

Most of this letter was later used in 2 Peter. Of note is the use of two Jewish works which were not accepted into the biblical canon: 1 Enoch (14-15) and the Assumption of Moses (9).

Revelation. The last book of the Bible is probably the one discussed most on a popular level among Christians, principally because of the emphasis radio and television evangelists give to it. The direction of the discussion is frequently flawed by treating the Book of Revelation as a coded prediction of the time of the end of the world. The book is also known as the Apocalypse, from its first word, *apocalypsis,* "revelation." It is in fact not the revelation of a new message or a secret design, but a presentation of the gospel in a different form. The author describes his work as a "prophetic message" (1:3; 22:10), which in biblical terminology is the authentic proclamation of the word of God.

The book was written in a literary form known as "apocalyptic" which flourished for about four centuries from 200 B.C. to A.D. 200. Apocalyptic typically contains dreams, angelic visions, signs and numerical symbols, and projections into the "future" (which is often the present from a past vantage point). Most of the symbols in the Book of Revelation have been interpreted by scholars with the aid of other literature of the period and are available in modern Catholic commentaries. Interpretation unaided by this knowledge results in fanciful application of the symbols to modern nations or events and in misrepresentation of the gospel message for today.

The Book of Revelation belongs to the branch of apocalyptic called "crisis literature" written to strengthen resistance and give hope and consolation in a time of danger. Revelation dates to the closing years of the reign of Domitian (A.D. 93-96), when Christians were persecuted for their faith throughout the

Roman empire. The author was John, a faithful Christian otherwise unknown to us, who had been exiled to the island of Patmos (off the coast of modern Turkey) because of his refusal to cooperate in pagan worship. He writes to seven churches of the mainland and through them to all believers to instill courage and fidelity in the time of crisis.

John draws heavily on biblical literature, particularly the books of Ezekiel and Daniel. Revelation includes quotations from or allusions to the Old Testament in 278 of its 404 verses. The Book of Daniel, crisis literature from an earlier time, is the source of the symbolic "a time, and times, and half a time" (12:14; Dn 7:25) or three and one-half years, a period which is also given as forty-two months or twelve hundred and sixty days (11:2-3). In Daniel this refers to the time of the Maccabean revolt, a three-and-one-half-year period of war and intense suffering between 167 and 164 B.C. In Revelation that time period symbolizes the whole life of the Church on earth as a time of suffering and persecution. A corresponding symbol, the one thousand years (20), represents the same period from the resurrection till the end of the world as a time of heavenly glory for the Church triumphant.

John opens his prophecy with a statement of the theme of hope and a description of his vision of the Lord as the Son of Man of Daniel 7. In chapters 2 and 3 he presents messages to the seven communities of Asia Minor in the form of letters from Jesus Christ. Each of these letters contains details applicable to the local congregation as well as a teaching for all Christians. These first three chapters are rich in scriptural allusion but contain very little arcane symbolism.

The central (and most difficult) section spans chapters 4 through 20. In a series of visions John gives the "signs" of the coming Day of the Lord. These visions of seals, trumpets, bowls, etc., are repetitious but involve a spiralling progress toward the final judgment in chapter 20. The struggle Christians experience is not essentially between their weak scattered communities and the mighty Roman empire but between the Church of Jesus Christ and Satan, between the Woman and the Dragon (12). The unholy trinity of the Dragon and the two beasts (his agents which represent the Roman empire—chapter 13) are allowed to harass the Church temporarily, but Jesus has already won the battle over evil and will soon establish his reign as King of Kings and Lord of Lords (19).

The final two chapters are an epilogue describing the Church as the new Jerusalem living in eternal splendor in heaven after the judgment and the destruction of God's enemies. John presents it to suffering Christians as a beacon of hope amid the raging persecution. He closes with Jesus' promise to come soon and with the response of the ancient Christian prayer, the Aramaic "Maranatha": "Come, Lord Jesus!"

NINE

Alongside the Testaments

Most of the books of the Old Testament were written by 300 B.C. During the last three hundred years before Christ these books were being added to the Old Testament canon based on their use in the Temple and synagogue. Three books from the third century B.C. (Esther, Ecclesiastes, and Tobit), four from the second (Sirach, Daniel, Judith, and 2 Maccabees), and three from the first (1 Maccabees, Baruch, Wisdom) would still find their way into the canon. But after the publication of Baruch and Wisdom around 50 B.C., the production of Jewish canonical writings ceased. A hundred years passed before the first canonical New Testament writing (1 Thessalonians) appeared.

Several noncanonical writings, some very similar in style and content to biblical books, have been preserved from that era. Occasionally the media carries stories of discoveries of parchment scrolls or fragments containing writings contemporaneous with the Bible. Many readers view such stories as interesting novelties and then toss them aside as of no pertinence. But the nonbiblical writings of the early Christian age have been and continue to be very helpful in the interpretation of the Hebrew and Christian Scriptures.

There was a literary continuity between the final writings of the Old Testament and the first Christian writings. There was not an abrupt end to one set of writings followed a century later by the abrupt beginning of the other. The transition took place within a context of continuing literary activity, as well as a regular flow of life in other areas. The first Christians were Jews; their writings are like other Jewish writings of the times but with a distinctive message and emphasis. Here I have assembled information about the most important noncanonical Jewish and Christian writings from this period. The material will help the Bible reader in gaining an awareness of the rich literary field behind the scriptural writings.

The Dead Sea Scrolls

The whole world knows about the discovery of the cache of ancient Hebrew scrolls in the Judean desert near the Dead Sea. In the spring of 1947 three teenage Bedouin boys were watching their goats on the rough slopes overlooking the northwest corner of the sea. One of them threw a stone into one of the many holes on the cliff face and heard the sound of shattering glass or pottery. On investigation, one of the boys found eight earthenware jars containing parchment scrolls. How these scrolls were evaluated, smuggled, sold, and deciphered is a detective story of high adventure. Eventually eleven caves in the area produced scrolls and thousands of fragments. They were written in Hebrew and Aramaic and contained Hebrew Scriptures, biblical commentaries, and other writings.

What are these scrolls? Where did they originate, and why were they in the caves? Both study of the script and accelerator mass spectrometry have confirmed the antiquity of the documents; they date from the fourth century B.C. to the first century A.D. They were found near the ruins of Qumran, where an ascetic sect of the Jews called Essenes had established a monastery. These scrolls were the library of the Essenes. They had been hidden in the caves for safekeeping ahead of the advance of the Roman army around A.D. 70. Members of the community hoped to return to retrieve the documents after the impending destruction, but for some reason were never able to do so. The scrolls remained in the caves, preserved by the arid climate for almost 2,000 years. The finds at Qumran stimulated further searches and led to the discovery of scrolls at other locations near the Dead Sea.

These scrolls are important for several reasons. Before this discovery, the earliest Hebrew manuscripts of the Old Testament books dated from around A.D. 1000. They were copies of copies handed down from antiquity. Scholars wondered how faithfully the texts had been transmitted over the centuries. When compared with the ancient scrolls from the Dead Sea, the texts from the Middle Ages were found to have preserved the ancient texts with remarkable accuracy. In many cases, however, where there was confusion about words, symbols, or usages in the later texts, the scrolls provided important clues to interpretation. The nonbiblical writings have been important for understanding language usage and religious thought.

The prize among the biblical writings discovered at Qumran is the complete scroll of the Book of Isaiah. It is now preserved at the Shrine of the Book in Jerusalem, built especially to house the Dead Sea Scrolls. The scrolls include extensive parts of other Old Testament books and some fragments, at least, of all the biblical books except Esther and the very latest productions (1 and 2 Maccabees, Judith, Baruch, Wisdom). Also found were fragments of Tobit in the hitherto lost Aramaic version. A few of the scrolls date back to the third century B.C., and are the oldest existing witnesses to the biblical text.

Among the nonbiblical writings are several commentaries on the Scriptures (Isaiah, Habakkuk, Psalms, Nahum) known by the technical name *pesharim* ("interpretations") because of their special technique of searching the text for applications to the life of the community at Qumran. Also discovered were original compositions similar to the biblical psalms (*Hymns of Thanksgiving*). Much information about the life of the Qumran community has been derived from the *Manual of Discipline* and from the *Zadokite Document* (also known as the *Damascus Document*). Their particular religious views are revealed in *The War of the Sons of Light and the Sons of Darkness*.

Ugarit and Ebla. Two other archeological discoveries of this century have come to have special bearing on the study of the Hebrew Scriptures, but not for the same reasons as the Dead Sea Scrolls. In the order of their appearance, the first is the discovery of the ancient city-state of Ugarit at Ras-Shamra on the northern coast of Syria (1928). Ugarit flourished for several hundred years before its destruction by the sea peoples about 1200 B.C. Its royal archives contained hundreds of tablets with texts in various languages, including Ugaritic, a language unknown before. The information about Canaanite religious myths in this library has filled in gaps of knowledge for Old Testament interpreters, and the Ugaritic language, a northwest Semitic dialect close to biblical Hebrew, illuminates various words and usages in the Bible.

Excavators at the inland site of Tell-Mardikh have identified the location as Ebla, the center of a far-flung and powerful empire of the third millenium B.C. which peaked in influence

2400-2250 B.C. More than 15,000 clay tablets have been unearthed. These are now being studied for their impact on biblical names, places, and practices, particularly those of the patriarchal period.

Apocryphal Writings

The problem caused by the different uses of the terms "apocrypha" and "pseudepigrapha" is discussed in chapter 4. Here "Apocryphal Writings" refers to books outside the biblical collection. The most important works from the period 200 B.C. to A.D. 200 are mentioned in this survey.

Writings Related to the Old Testament

Books of Enoch (150 B.C.- A.D. 200). The figure of the patriarch Enoch exercised a powerful attraction among the Hebrews: "The whole lifetime of Enoch was three hundred and sixty-five years. Then Enoch walked with God, and he was no longer here, for God took him" (Gn 5:23-24). In the Bible he is referred to as a model servant of God who was taken bodily into heaven (Sir 44:16; 49:14); he was our forerunner in faith (Heb 11:5) and a forefather of Jesus (Lk 3:37). A literature attributed to him originated in the postexilic period.

The most important document is 1 Enoch (150-100 B.C.), called Ethiopic Enoch because of the language in which it was preserved (though the original was Aramaic). The patriarch relates the story of the Fall and foretells the Flood and other coming events. He describes the coming of the Messiah, a heavenly being called the Son of Man. Second Enoch, or Slavonic Enoch (A.D. 70), tells of the patriarch's journey through heaven and hell. This book was edited by Christians in its transmission. A third work, 3 Enoch or Hebrew Enoch, is a mystical writing from the second century A.D. or later.

Book of Jubilees (150-125 B.C.). The Book of Jubilees is also known as the Apocalypse of Moses because it claims to have been presented to Moses on Sinai as a revelation concerning the history of the world, the eternal validity of the Law, and certain doctrinal issues current during the last part of the second century B.C. This book contains one of the earliest references in Palestine to the doctrine of immortality. Fragments of eleven manuscripts of the work were found at Qumran, a witness to its importance a century or two after its composition.

Letter of Aristeas (second century B.C.). The writer of this letter, composed in Alexandria in Greek, presents himself as an officer in the court of Ptolemy II Philadelphus of Egypt (283-247 B.C.), writing for the spiritual edification of his brother Philocrates. This is the most positive Jewish statement of the time on Greek culture and the possibility of successful ecumenical relations between Jewish and Greek religions. The Letter of Aristeas is the source of the legend about the translation of the Hebrew Scriptures into Greek by seventy-two scholars in seventy-two days. The name for the Greek Old Testament, *Septuagint* ("seventy"), also derives from this book.

Testaments of the Twelve Patriarchs (second century B.C.). The "last testament" form is well known in the Bible: Jacob's blessing of his twelve sons (Gn 49); Moses' blessing of the tribes before the entry into Canaan (Dt 33); Jesus' last discourse (Jn 13-17). This work contains the blessings of the twelve patriarchs over their sons.

Books of Esdras (100 B.C.- A.D. 200). Confusion surrounds the name given to these books because, besides the two apocryphal books of Esdras, the two biblical books of Ezra and Nehemiah were known as 1 and 2 Esdras in Catholic Bibles based on the Latin Vulgate. Today the name *1 Esdras* is reserved for a noncanonical writing of around 100 B.C. It borrows heavily from the biblical books of 2 Chronicles, Ezra, and Nehemiah. The main addition is the story of a competition at the Persian court in which Zerubbabel won the right to lead the Jews back to Jerusalem after the Babylonian Exile. The apocryphal 2 Esdras is a composite of three different writings dating from the last part of the first century A.D. and later. A Jewish writing lamenting the destruction of Jerusalem in A.D. 70 is enclosed by a Christian introduction from the second century A.D. and a Christian conclusion from the third century. Though not considered "deuterocanonical" books by Catholics, 1 and 2 Esdras are treated as "apocrypha" by Protestants and are often published in interdenominational Bibles.

3 and 4 Maccabees (100 B.C.- A.D. 50). Third Maccabees (100 B.C.) is not about the Maccabees, but tells of a Jewish conflict with the Egyptian King Ptolemy IV Philopator in the late third century B.C. Most of the material is legendary, composed by an Alexandrian Jew to encourage fidelity in case of Roman persecution. Fourth Maccabees was probably also written in Alexandria, but more than a hundred years later. It presents a philosophical argument proving the supremacy of reason over human passion, especially the power of faith-filled reason to overcome suffering and persecution.

Psalms of Solomon (50 B.C.). This collection of eighteen psalms was composed by Jews in Palestine and was similar enough to the biblical collection to be accepted as canonical in some localities. A major theme centers around the punishment of Israel by God for the worldliness of its leaders. The theme may reflect the hostility of the Essenes (such as those at Qumran) to the ruling high priests.

Assumption of Moses (A.D. 30). A Jewish writer reacting to the Roman oppression of Israel conceived this book (also known as the Testament of Moses) as the final instruction of Moses to Joshua. The book "foresees" events leading up to the author's own time, which is believed to be very close to the dawn of the end-time.

Martyrdom of Isaiah (A.D. 100). This book is the source of the story that the prophet Isaiah was sawed in two by command of the wicked King Manasseh of Judah (687-642 B.C.). Later Christian writers added to this a vision of Isaiah which foresees the birth, death, and resurrection of Jesus.

Books of Baruch (A.D. 80-200). Baruch, the secretary of Jeremiah (Jer 45:1), was, like Enoch, a popular figure in the Jewish imagination. Besides the canonical Book of Baruch (50 B.C.), two apocryphal books of Baruch appear among the later Hebrew writings. Second Baruch (or the Syriac Apocalypse of Baruch) was written after the fall of Jerusalem toward the end of the first century A.D. The scene is set after the earlier fall of

Jerusalem to Babylon in 587 B.C. Baruch is given visions explaining the reasons for the tragedy. He foresees the messianic age and the resurrection of the dead. Third Baruch (the Greek Apocalypse), the story of Baruch's journey through the seven heavens, was written by a Jew in the second century A.D. and later revised by a Christian editor.

Prayer of Manasseh (A.D. 100). This is a beautiful penitential psalm composed as the prayer of King Manasseh of Judah mentioned in 2 Chronicles 33:18. It appears as a canticle attached to the Psalms in some Greek and Latin manuscripts. Like 1 and 2 Esdras, this prayer is contained among the "Apocrypha" in interdenominational Bibles, though it is not considered deuterocanonical by Catholics.

Sibylline Oracles (second century A.D.). The pagan prophetess Sibyl of Cumae (500 B.C.) was the model for "sibyls" throughout the ancient Hellenistic world—women through whom the gods revealed their oracles. The Jews imitated the pagans in composing their own sibylline oracles beginning about 200 B.C. In these, the sibyls foresaw the history of the Jews and the coming of the messianic age. Christians later added some oracles foreshadowing the life of Christ. The present collection was assembled about A.D. 500.

Writings Related to the New Testament

Beginning in the second century A.D., Christian writers produced numerous writings imitating and paralleling the canonical books of the New Testament. They wrote gospels, acts, epistles, and apocalypses. Most of these productions are fanciful, created to fill in the blanks and gaps of the biblical writings. Some of the legendary details still have their influence today. The rare pieces of reliable material that might supplement the information given in the canonical books are found in the apocryphal gospels. Only a small selection from the vast field will be given here.

Gospels

Gospel of Peter (A.D. 150). The Gospel of Peter, referred to by some of the early Church Fathers, is available to us only in the part discovered in Upper Egypt in 1886. It was compiled from the four canonical gospels, but adds details and commentary to prove the validity of the Christian faith. The Resurrection is pictured as taking place before pagan and Jewish witnesses. The description of the Passion is tinged with Docetism (which denied the reality of Jesus' human body).

Gospel of Thomas (A.D. 150). This is the most important of the New Testament apocrypha. The Gospel of Thomas is a collection of 114 sayings of Jesus with very little narrative. Some of the sayings are identical or parallel to passages in the canonical gospels; most of them are not, and may contain authentic material, though the document has Gnostic overtones. This gospel was discovered along with forty-three other works in 1945-46 near the village of Nag-Hammadi in Egypt; the books were probably part of the library of the monastery founded by St. Pachomius (A.D. 320).

Gospel of the Hebrews (second century A.D.). Two works that go by this name are known only by references and citations in the writings of early Church Fathers. One of them may be related to the canonical Gospel of Matthew. The other was composed in Egypt and contains some interesting variants on canonical gospel stories. It was written for Jewish Christians, as was another work called the Gospel of the Ebionites written around the same time.

Protevangelium of James (A.D. 150). This infancy gospel is of little historical value, but has had great influence on the popular imagination through the centuries. The Protevangelium of James is the source of the childhood stories about Mary's birth and dedication in the Temple, the names of her parents, the idea that Joseph was a widower and miraculously chosen to be her husband. It is one of the earliest witnesses to Christian Marian piety.

Other Gospels. Besides the works described above, there exist gospels attributed to the Twelve as a group, and several to individuals: Philip, John, Bartholomew, Matthias, even Judas. There is a Gospel of Nicodemus, and a History of Joseph the Carpenter. Most of these date from the fourth century or later. A book entitled The Assumption of the Virgin, composed in the seventh century, brings the apostles back on clouds to witness the glorious end of Mary's life.

Acts

The works described here illustrate the general trend of this apocryphal literature. Other works include: Acts of John, Andrew, Thomas, and Philip, to name a few. These writings often exhibit strains of Docetism and of Encratism (a rigid ascetical doctrine outlawing marriage).

Acts of Paul (A.D. 160). The letters of Paul and the story of his journeys in Acts leave much room for speculation about his activities during times not accounted for. The Acts of Paul coordinates its new (imaginary) information with the data in the New Testament. A major section recounts Paul's conversion of Thecla, a disciple from Iconium in Asia Minor, and her subsequent activities, including a miraculous escape from the beasts in the arena. These Acts also contain a story of Paul's martyrdom in his Roman prison and his apparition to Emperor Nero.

Acts of Pilate (A.D. 200). Several legendary stories about Pilate and his reputed conversion to Christianity arose in the second century. Justin Martyr (A.D. 150) refers to some of these tales. The Acts of Pilate was compiled to substantiate the resurrection of Jesus and to answer various charges of Christian opponents; for example, when Mary is accused of adultery because she was with child before marriage, some devout Jews come forward to attest that she was a virgin at the time they witnessed the wedding of Mary and Joseph.

Acts of Peter (A.D. 200). The longest part of this work deals with a confrontation between Simon the magician (known from Acts 8:9-24) and Peter in Jerusalem. Also included is a short section on the daughter of Peter, and most importantly for popular Christian tradition, the story of Quo Vadis, Peter's meeting with Jesus as the apostle was fleeing Rome.

Letter of Barnabas (A.D. 130). The earliest and most significant of the apocryphal letters is this homiletic treatise attributed to the companion of St. Paul. The author expresses concern about Judaizing influences among Christians, as Paul had in his letter to the Galatians. Barnabas' approach, however, is violently anti-Jewish. Paul recognized the covenant and the Hebrew Scriptures as God's work, but "Barnabas" considers the Old Testament a work of the devil.

Apocalypse of Peter (A.D. 130). This writing presents visions of the beatitude of the Christian saints in heaven and the punishment of sinners in hell. Its vivid description of the torments of the damned has been compared to scenes in Dante's *Divine Comedy*. The question of this book's canonicity was still being debated at the end of the second century (see Muratorian Canon below).

Other Jewish Writings

Mention will be made here of other Jewish sources which are often brought to bear on questions of biblical interpretation or historicity.

Philo. Philo was a Jewish philosopher of Alexandria (25 B.C.-A.D. 41). He brought together in his writings his own Jewish tradition and the Greek culture of the times. He is the best witness we have of the Jewish approach to Hellenism at the dawn of Christianity. It is debatable whether he influenced the New Testament writings, but he was read and quoted by Christian theologians into the Middle Ages.

Flavius Josephus. This Jewish historian is our principal non-biblical source of information about Palestine and Judaism during the time of Jesus. Flavius Josephus was born in Palestine in A.D. 37 or 38, joined the Pharisees as a young man, and in 66 became commander of the Jewish forces in Galilee for the revolt against Rome. After the Romans killed most of his regiment at Jotapata in 67, Josephus surrendered to the Roman general, Vespasian. He attached himself to Vespasian and his son, Titus, both of whom would become emperors, and took their family name, Flavius.

Josephus went to Rome with Titus after the Roman victory over Jerusalem in 70; he was given Roman citizenship and an imperial pension. Josephus' most important works are *The Jewish War* (7 books), detailing the unsuccessful revolt against Rome, and *Antiquities of the Jews* (20 books), the history of the Jews from the creation of the world until the time of Emperor Nero. Josephus died in Rome about the year 100.

Rabbinic Literature. From early times in Judaism, the rabbis (teachers) interpreted the Law and applied it to the needs of succeeding generations. In the popular imagination, this oral law was believed to have been handed down from Moses and to carry his authority. After the destruction of the Temple in A.D. 70, the rabbis, under Johanan ben Zakkai, initiated an intensive program to collect and organize the oral maxims of earlier teachers. Rabbi Judah ha-Nasi finally codified this work in written form at the end of the second century. His work, called the *Mishnah,* achieved such authoritative status that it became a primary object of rabbinical commentary itself.

The *Mishnah* became the core of the *Talmud,* the main collection of Jewish rabbinical teaching. In the years after the appearance of the *Mishnah,* rabbis discussed it in the "academies" in Palestine and Babylonia. Their opinions, called the *Gemara,* were published with the *Mishnah* to make up the *Talmud* about A.D. 500. Other major rabbinic resources are *the Tosephta,* early opinions left out of the *Mishnah,* and *Midrash,* homiletic commentaries on the biblical text.

Though the material in these collections was not written down till well after the biblical period, it often reflects customs and teaching current during the early Christian period and before, and therefore can sometimes help in interpretation.

Other Christian Writings

Unlike the apocrypha, which copied the biblical style and were artificially promoted as writings of New Testament figures or their friends, other early Christian writings merit greater attention. Some were considered canonical for awhile in various parts of the early Church. The few mentioned here are those which are occasionally referred to in questions of New Testament commentary or canonicity.

The Didache (A.D. 90-100). *The Teaching of the Twelve Apostles* is known by the first word of its Greek title, which means "teaching." Written in Syria while some of the last books of the New Testament were still being produced, the *Didache* is of enormous importance for its witness to the liturgical practice and moral teaching of the early Christians. It contains (1) a moral catechism known as the Book of the Two Ways, (2) a liturgical instruction dealing with baptism, prayer and fasting, and the Eucharist, (3) disciplinary regulations about teachers and traveling prophets, and (4) an exhortation concerning the second coming of Christ.

The Letters of Clement (A.D. 96). St. Clement is revered as the fourth bishop of Rome, successor to Saints Peter, Linus, and Anacletus, on the basis of the information in St. Irenaeus' *Adversus Haereses* (A.D. 200). Two *Letters to the Corinthians* passed down to us under his name, and both were considered Scripture at one time or another. Only one of these letters, *1 Clement*, is authentic. It was written shortly after the persecution under the Emperor Domitian (A.D. 81-96), which ended in 95 or 96. The first part exhorts readers to a life of Christian virtue; the second consists of admonitions and directions for healing rifts in the community at Corinth caused by agitators. Clement urges obedience to the appointed leaders. This letter is important in the history of Roman primacy: Clement intervened in the affairs of Corinth without being invited to, and his letter was so well received that it was still being read in Corinthian churches seventy years later.

The document known as *2 Clement* is a homily written between A.D. 125 and 150. Though it was falsely attributed to St. Clement of Rome, this work is the oldest extant nonbiblical Christian sermon and is an example of early moral teaching.

The Letters of Ignatius of Antioch (A.D. 110). St. Ignatius became bishop of Antioch in Syria, the important missionary center where Paul and Barnabas had been active (Acts 11:19-30; 13:1-3). He is a strong witness to the early emergence of episcopal church order. Ignatius was taken to Rome for martyrdom in about A.D. 110 during the reign of Emperor Trajan (98-117). On this journey he wrote seven letters: to the churches of Ephesus, Magnesia, Tralles, Rome, Philadelphia, and Smyrna, and to St. Polycarp, the bishop of Smyrna. These letters are treasured for their strong expression of faith and intense yearning for Christ.

The Odes of Solomon (early second century A.D.). This collection of 42 odes by a Christian well versed in Jewish literature combines the flavor of the Hebrew Psalter with faith that the Messiah has already come. Scholars have noted similarities with the Gospel of John and the Qumran documents and use the Odes in studying the origins of New Testament thought.

The Shepherd of Hermas (A.D. 150). Hermas was the brother of Pope Pius I (A.D. 140-155). He composed his apocalyptic book, *The Shepherd,* in Rome during his brother's pontificate. Hermas was scandalized by the laxity he saw among Christians, and he was determined to call them back to penance and a life of virtue. The book begins with a series of four visions in which Hermas is visited by a woman in a white dress, the Church, who becomes progressively younger. She tells Hermas of his own need for penance and of his mission to spread the message to others. In the fifth vision, the Angel of Penance appears to him in the form of a shepherd who delivers a series of mandates and instructions which make up the rest of the book. *The Shepherd* provides important information about the early stages of the Church's teaching and practice of repentance and conversion. It was treated as Scripture in some areas at least until the time of Origen (185-253).

Diatessaron (A.D. 175). The author of this unique work was a Syrian named Tatian, who came to Rome and became a Christian and a disciple of St. Justin. The *Diatessaron* ("through four") is a harmony of the four Gospels created by editing them into a single continuous narrative. It was popular enough in Syria to be incorporated in the Syriac liturgy.

Muratorian Canon (A.D. 200). This, the oldest existing list of the books of the New Testament, takes its name from L.A. Muratori, who discovered the manuscript copy in the Ambrosian Library in 1740. The canon was probably drawn up to counteract the spread of Gnostic literature in the church of Rome. Differences from our present canon are these: missing from the list are Hebrews, James, 1 and 2 Peter, and one of the Letters of John, probably 3 John; added are the Book of Wisdom (as a part of the New Testament instead of the Old) and, with reservations, the apocryphal Apocalypse of Peter. Two apocryphal letters attributed to St. Paul, to the Alexandrians and the Laodiceans, are rejected by name. *The Shepherd of Hermas* is recommended for public reading, but not as a book of Scripture.

TEN

In the Days of Jesus

A full-scale presentation of the social setting of the biblical writings would include Palestine during the succeeding stages of its history, Babylon during the Exile, and the Mediterranean world of the Roman empire into the second century A.D. Our scope here is limited to political and religious factors found in the Palestine of the first century A.D. up to the fall of Jerusalem in 70. The historical information in chapter 5 may provide helpful background for understanding the political situation of Palestine described here.

Land

The size of Palestine varied during biblical times, but its classical dimensions are Dan in the north to Beer-sheba in the south (2 Sm 3:10) between the Mediterranean Sea and the Jordan River. The distance from north to south covers about 150 miles (roughly the same as from Washington to Philadelphia or Austin to Houston), from east to west 50 miles. The area is about that of New Jersey. Most people travelled on foot at a pace of about twenty miles a day.

The land divides into three geographical terrains. To the west is the plain bordering the sea. The Carmel range juts out to the sea to form the harbor at Haifa; south of this are the fertile areas of Sharon and the Shephelah. In the center of the country, like a backbone, stands a ridge of hills running north and south. To the east lies the Jordan valley. Near the Jordan the land is some-times fertile, but much of this lowland is wilderness. Around the Dead Sea it turns into desert.

The political and religious center of Palestine was Jerusalem in the southern province of Judea. Many of the Jews here descended from the pioneers who returned from the Babylonian Exile in the sixth century B.C. The geographical center of the country was Samaria. The Samaritans observed the Law of Moses and wanted to think of themselves as full-fledged Jews, but the establishment Jews of Judea considered them renegades because they had intermarried with foreigners and (in despera-tion) built their own temple. Galilee was in the north, united with Judea in religion but separated by the hostile presence of Samaria between them. This was and is the most fertile of the provinces. The Sea of Galilee is a fresh-water lake eight miles wide and twelve miles long. The region was called "Galilee of the Gentiles" (Mt 4:15) because of the many non-Jews who dwelt there. Galilean Jews made up for their distance from the Jerusalem Temple by religious zeal and tenacity.

Political Situation

Pompey's conquest of Palestine in 63 B.C. ended a period of Jewish independence and brought the nation under Roman control as part of the province of Syria. Herod the Great showed adroit political skill in surviving upheavals in imperial leadership during the mid-first century B.C. He began to reign in 37 B.C. as the king of Judea directly under the emperor without the Roman legate in Syria as intermediary authority. The Jews had always been jealous of their independence as God's people. They chafed under Roman domination, and Herod's appointment did little to lessen the tension. The Romans looked on Herod as a Jew, but to the Jews themselves he was an interloper, an Idumean with Semitic blood but no religious faith.

At Herod's death in 4 B.C., his kingdom was divided among three of his sons: Archelaus ruled the key area of Judea and Samaria, Antipas ruled Galilee and Perea (in Transjordan), and Philip ruled the Decapolis east of the Sea of Galilee. These political divisions remained during the ministry of Jesus, except that Archelaus had been removed in A.D. 6 for mismanagement and replaced by a Roman governor, called a "prefect" and later a "procurator." The procurator held full jurisdiction over his territory, gathering taxes for Rome, insuring the peace, and deciding in cases of capital punishment. The Bible mentions three governors—the prefect Pontius Pilate (A.D. 25-36) in the Gospels, and the procurators M. Antonius Felix (52-60) and Porcius Festus (60-62) in the Acts of the Apostles.

Some Jews supported Rome. The most outspoken were the group known as the Herodians, supporters of the family of Herod in their unswerving loyalty to Rome. At the opposite extreme were the Zealots, a revolutionary group dedicated to the ousting of Rome from Palestine. The Zealot reaction had been precipitated by the imperial census under Quirinius in A.D. 6. Agents of the group committed acts of terrorism against Roman soldiers and against Jews they considered Roman sympathizers. The Zealots initiated the rebellion which ended in the destruction of Jerusalem and the Temple in A.D. 70. Simon the

Zealot, one of the Twelve (Lk 6:15), was probably a former member of this group.

Anti-Roman sentiments were kept seething especially through the system of taxation. Herod the Great taxed the Jews heavily to finance his vast construction operations. After his death, a delegation of the Jews went to the emperor to ask that Herod's sons not be allowed to continue the exorbitant taxes, but their plea was ineffective. Conditions became even worse in the eyes of many Jews in A.D. 6, when the newly appointed Roman governor introduced Roman taxes. Now not only were the taxes heavy, they were paid to a foreign power.

The Romans applied two kinds of direct tax and many indirect taxes. The direct taxes were a property tax and a personal, or poll, tax (Rom 13:7). Jesus was questioned about the lawfulness of this poll, or census, tax (Mk 12:13-17). The indirect taxes included mostly tolls at crossroads, bridges, entries into towns and marketplaces. The state employed tax gatherers who were charged a fixed sum for a particular territory. The tax collectors then set the rates in order to pay this charge and enrich themselves. The abuses encouraged by this system only increased hostility toward Rome. Matthew, one of the Twelve, was a tax collector (Mt 9:9).

Religious Groups

Several religious groups and institutions in the Judaism of Jesus' time are reflected in the Gospels. They include Pharisees and Sadducces (Mt 3:7), scribes (Lk 5:30), lawyers (Lk 7:30), a high priest (Jn 11:49), chief priests and elders (Mk 14:53), priests and Levites (Lk 10:31-32), and an official body called the

Sanhedrin (Mk 14:55). In addition, discoveries at Qumran have focused attention on a Jewish group called the Essenes. What was the nature of these various religious elements?

The Gospels frequently mention the Pharisees as opponents of Jesus. They were a lay group which originated as a reform movement within Judaism during the Hasmonean dynasty about 150 B.C. The Pharisees opposed Hellenistic adaptations in Judaism and especially the politicizing of the high priesthood in the time of John Hyrcanus (134-104 B.C.) and his successors. Their name, which means "Separated Ones," probably began as a nickname imposed by their opponents. Like the names "Christian" and "Puritan" later on, this name became accepted as a mark of honor.

The Pharisees were very popular with the ordinary people and were looked up to as holy examples of religious observance. They vigorously interpreted the Law, which for them meant not only the first five books of the Bible (the Torah), but many other holy writings and the oral interpretations which had been passed down by earlier teachers. Their legalism in the applications of the 613 prescriptions and prohibitions of the Torah brought them into conflict with Jesus.

The Sadducees were the aristocratic ruling class who controlled the Temple. Many of them were priests. Unlike the Pharisees, the Sadducees were generally despised by the common people. They favored the rule of Rome which guaranteed the continuation of their authority, and they allowed latitude in adapting to political realities and Hellenistic patterns. The Sadducees accepted only the first five books of the Bible as authoritative, rejecting some teachings which were fundamental to the beliefs of the Pharisees: resurrection of the body, the existence and activity of angels, God's active involvement in daily affairs (see Mk 12:18-27; Acts 23:6-10). In general, the Sadducees were more secular than religious.

The institution of the scribes, or expert teachers of the Law, developed after the Babylonian Exile, and grew stronger in reaction to the persecution by the Seleucid overlords. The scribes set up schools of instruction and were addressed by the title "Rabboni" ("my master"). The Gospel of Luke sometimes calls them "lawyers." At the time of Jesus most of the scribes were Pharisees. The grouping "scribes and Pharisees" is familiar in the Gospels, but not "scribes and Sadducees."

According to the Book of Exodus, at the time of Moses the priesthood was awarded to the tribe of Levi for its fidelity (Ex 32:25-29). But other texts make it clear that it was not all the Levites but only the family of Aaron which was set aside to offer the sacrifices (Ex 40:12-15; Lv 8). This was later limited to one family within the clan of Aaron, the sons of Zadok (Ez 40:46). At the time of Jesus, only certain members of the Zadok (Sadducee) family, who were able to prove their qualifications for the office, were accepted into the priesthood. The other members of the tribe of Levi (the "Levites") were assigned the secondary duties of providing for the cleaning and upkeep of the Temple, arranging material for the services, and guarding the precincts.

The position of head or high priest came into prominence after the Exile. During the Hasmonean era, the offices of high priest and king were combined (1 Mc 14:41-47). In Jesus' time the high priest possessed extensive power as supervisor of the official religion, and exclusive rights and duties in the Temple ritual. High priests were appointed to their office by Rome and had to preserve their place by assuring good order and loyalty among the people. Some high priests held office for only brief periods but maintained prestige and influence after they were deposed. This explains the plural "high priests" or "chief priests." The family of Annas produced several high priests over a period of almost six decades. Annas himself held office from A.D. 7 to 11. His son-in-law Caiaphas, high priest during the trial of Jesus, held office almost continuously from 18 to 36, while five of Annas' sons were high priests at various times up until 63. Annas evidently still held great power long after his tenure in office. John reports that at his trial Jesus was taken to Annas first, then to Caiaphas (Jn 18:13, 24). Luke refers to both Annas and Caiaphas as high priests at the beginning of the ministry of John the Baptist (Lk 3:2).

The high priest presided over the Sanhedrin, the supreme council of the Jews composed of seventy-one members, in memory of the tradition of Moses and the seventy elders (Nm 11:16-17). In the time of Jesus, membership in the Sanhedrin was distributed among members of the high priestly families, the elders (influential members of the Jewish community), and the scribes (Lk 22:66). Small councils to decide local matters required a minimum membership of 120 men (Acts 1:15).

The Essenes, another major group among the Jews of Jesus' time, remained outside the structures just described and were aloof from the ordinary religious life of the country. They adhered strictly to the Law of Moses and separated themselves from the mainstream of religious observance, living in various enclaves throughout the land. The largest group probably lived at Qumran on the Dead Sea, where the famous Dead Sea Scrolls were discovered (see chapter 8). The Essenes of Jesus' time, never mentioned in the New Testament, were the heirs of the Jews who split away from the Temple when Jonathan Maccabeus, a non-Zadokite, accepted appointment as high priest (152 B.C.: 1 Mc 10:18-21).

All of the Jews of Jesus' time were looking for the promised age of salvation. They had different views about the "anointed of the Lord" (Messiah) who would signal and inaugurate this final era. Many looked for a new David, who would resurrect Jewish hopes by political and military might. The Essenes expected such an anointed king and a second figure, an anointed priest who would reestablish the fallen priesthood of Israel. The expectation of a prophet like Moses (Dt 18:18) is reflected in the Baptist's explanation of his role in John 1:21. Jesus understood his messianic mission in terms of the servant of Isaiah (Is 52:13-53:12).

Temple and Synagogue

The religious life of Jews in Jesus' time revolved around the Temple and the synagogue, two distinct institutions. The Temple in Jerusalem was the place of sacrifices which only priests could perform. There were many synagogues, however, places for meeting, prayer, reading, and interpretation of the Scriptures.

The first Temple, built by King Solomon in between 967 and 961 B.C. (1 Kgs 6), was the pride of Israel. Eventually, the Temple became so identified with God's presence that some felt it could not be destroyed. Its destruction by the Babylonians in 587 B.C. thus shattered much more than the building. The returned exiles built a new Temple under the urging of the prophets Haggai and Zechariah (520-515 B.C.: Ezr 5-6). The new Temple suffered plunder and profanation at the hands of Antiochus IV Epiphanes (169-167 B.C.: 1 Mc 1:20-59) but was rededicated by the Maccabees (1 Mc 4:36-59). By the time of

Herod the Great (37 B.C.-A.D. 4), the Temple was in need of major repair. Probably for political more than religious reasons, Herod inaugurated a rebuilding program in 20 B.C. The major construction was completed in ten years, but the decoration and finishing work went on until A.D. 63, only a few years before the complete destruction of the Temple by the Romans.

The Herodian Temple was modeled as much as possible on the Temple of Solomon. Herod expanded the Temple courts by filling and walling a large rectangular area. The court of the women was a large gathering place containing alms boxes for the poor. West of this was the Court of Israel, which only Jewish males could enter, and beyond this the Court of the Priests containing the altar of holocausts (burnt offerings). Each of these courts stood a few steps higher than the last. At a still higher level stood the sanctuary, an impressive building of massive white stones. Its vestibule was twelve steps above the Court of the Priests. Behind this was the Holy Place with the altar of incense, the table of the showbread (twelve loaves, renewed each sabbath, representing the twelve tribes), and the seven-branched candlestick. Each one of the twenty-four units of priests performed the offering of the incense twice a year for one week at a time (Lk 1:8). The most sacred part of the Temple was the Holy of Holies, separated from the Holy Place by a sacred curtain. The high priest entered the Holy of Holies only once a year on the Day of Atonement. The Holy of Holies had originally contained the Ark of the Covenant (which disappeared at the time of the Exile), but by Jesus' time contained only a black stone altar for incense.

The Temple area was ringed by a large open court, with the largest expanse to the south, called the Court of the Gentiles. Anyone could enter here, but a gentile was forbidden to enter the other courts under penalty of death; and introducing a gentile into a restricted area was considered a criminal profanation (Acts 21:28). This "outer temple" resembled a town square. Its colonnades provided places for arguments about the Law, the purchase of sacrificial animals, and the exchange of secular currency for ritually clean coinage.

Besides the offerings of personal piety by the constant stream of pilgrims to the Temple, there were two official holocausts—whole burnt offerings—each day. After the sacrifice of the lamb in the morning, a priest would stand on the steps above the Court of Israel to recite the *Shema,* the traditional daily prayer from Deuteronomy 6:4-5, and to read a passage of the Law. The mid-afternoon sacrifice was accompanied by the blessing of Aaron:

> The Lord bless you and keep you!
> The Lord let his face shine upon you, and be gracious to you!
> The Lord look upon you kindly and give you peace!
>
> NUMBERS 6:24-26

The synagogue differed from the Temple. Prayer and instruction, but not sacrifice, were the focus of its observances. The historical origin of this institution is disputed, but we know that synagogues were functioning three centuries before Christ. They probably arose in response to the worship needs of Jews separated from the Temple by exile or migration. Synagogues were present in every village; larger towns had more than one. The Jerusalem of Jesus' time contained more than 300 synagogues, some of them of course very small. These might have been organized on the basis of neighborhood, nationality, or profession. Jewish children were trained in the synagogues; in the villages, synagogues housed town meetings.

The synagogue was constructed as a faint model of the Jerusalem Temple. It included a court open to all and a central chamber for prayer and reading of the Law. Instead of a Holy of Holies an "ark" was set apart usually in an apse. This ark contained the Torah and other scrolls and the trumpets used to proclaim the holy days. A lamp burned continually before the door or curtain shielding the ark.

A priestly office was not connected with the synagogue. A council of ten elders elected a president to supervise the services, instruction, and upkeep. Prayers were offered daily in the synagogue, but on the Sabbath a more developed service was offered. This began with a prayer said facing Jerusalem; then the reading of the Law was given according to a three-year cycle. The lector could then make a commentary on the text (Lk 4:16-21). The meeting closed with prayer and benediction

The Calendar and the Feasts

The fact that the Jews followed a solar calendar for the year (365 days) but a lunar calendar for the months (354 days for twelve months) complicated the system of reckoning dates. Every two or three years an extra month was added in the following way. After the month Adar (February-March), a committee of doctors of the Law checked the prospects for the barley harvest, which had to begin before the feast of Passover on the fifteenth of Nisan, the first month of the year. If more time were needed, the doctors proclaimed a thirteenth month, Second Adar.

The Israelites adopted the Canaanite names for the months when they first occupied the land. A few of these names still appear in the Old Testament, but Israel used the Babylonian months from the time of the Exile:

Nisan	March-April
Iyyar	April-May
Siwan	May-June
Tammuz	June-July
Ab	July-August
Elul	August-September
Tishri	September-October
Marheshwan	October-November
Kisleu	November-December
Tebet	December-January
Shebat	January-February
Adar	February-March

Along with these names, the Israelites had adopted the Babylonian custom of beginning the year in the spring month of Nisan. But they also maintained the older custom of celebrating the new year in the fall month of Tishri so that the Old Testament reflects both practices.

The Jewish day began at sunset: "Thus evening came, and morning followed—the first day" (Gn 1:5). The officials insisted that Jesus' body be removed before sunset Friday because after that the work of burial would have broken the Sabbath observance (Jn 19:31). The day was divided into twelve hours, the night into four watches. The duration of these time units varied according to the seasons of the year.

The division of the month into weeks of seven days may date back to Mesopotamian observation of the phases of the moon, but the institution of the Sabbath is from the Hebrews. The

Sabbath was not just a day to rest from work on the seventh day. It was a memorial of the covenant and a celebration of God's loving relationship with his people. It was an act of faith in his provident care. By the time of Jesus, the laws protecting the Sabbath had spawned restrictive minutiae. These observances replaced the carefree atmosphere of a time for thankful prayer and leisure with a more oppressive mood. Jesus' attempts to return to the original purpose of the Sabbath touched the nerve center of his opposition (Mk 2:23-3:6).

Friday was a day of preparation for the Sabbath: the gathering of necessary supplies, preparation of food, cleaning. At sunset a trumpet signaled the beginning of the Sabbath. Then the lamps were lit and the evening meal began with the blessing of wine and herbs. After this, no one ate till after the synagogue service the next morning. Often the doctors of the Law would discuss important questions in the afternoon. The evening meal, accompanied by blessings, took place late in the afternoon and was often interrupted by the trumpet signaling the end of the Sabbath.

Various feasts of the year punctuated the regular Sabbath observance. These included three week-long pilgrimage feasts during which, ideally, Jews were to come to the Jerusalem Temple: Passover, Pentecost, and Tabernacles (Ex 34:22-23).

Passover, a spring festival (month of Nisan), commemorated the liberation of the Israelites from Egypt at the Exodus. It was combined with the Feast of the Unleavened Bread which celebrated the beginning of the barley harvest. Elements of both feasts appear in the observances. All leavened bread was removed from Jewish houses before the preparation of the unleavened barley cakes to be eaten during the festival. A paschal lamb, the first and best of the flock, was sacrificed in the

Temple and then shared at home in the Passover meal with meaningful ritual recalling the slavery in Egypt and the Exodus.

Pentecost, the Feast of the Grain Harvest (month of Siwan); (Ex 23:16), was celebrated seven weeks after Passover (and for this reason was also called the Feast of Weeks). Its name comes from the Greek for "fiftieth day." The observance centered on the offering of the first loaves made from the new wheat. Eventually this feast was celebrated as the anniversary of the giving of the Law on Mount Sinai.

The Feast of Tabernacles, or Tents or Booths, was also called the Feast of Ingathering (Ex 23:16) because it took place at the completion of the autumn harvest (month of Tishri). This was the most important of the pilgrimage festivals, sometimes even called "the feast" (Ez 45:25). It was also the most popular, because the work of harvest was over and people were free to relax. A special feature of this feast was the use of huts made of branches as a place to live during the seven days of the celebration. This imitated the living conditions of harvest workers, and also commemorated the homelessness of the ancient Israelites during the wandering in the desert. Every morning during Tabernacles, a special ceremonial procession accompanied a priest to the pool of Siloam where he filled a golden pitcher with water to pour out on the altar of sacrifice in the Temple. Every evening the Court of the Women was lit up by the fire of great candlesticks and a select group of men performed a dance with torches. It was during this feast that Jesus spoke of himself as the source of living water and the light of the world (Jn 7:37-39; 8:12).

Three other feasts were of special significance for the Jews of Jesus' time. Yom Kippur (Day of Atonement) falls on the tenth of Tishri, a few days before Tabernacles. It was a day of strict fasting. The high priest entered the Holy of Holies with sacrificial blood and later, by a symbolic imposition of hands, transferred the sins of the community to a goat (scapegoat) which was then released into the desert (Lv 16:20-28). Hannukah (Dedication), celebrated on the twenty-fifth of Kisleu (November-December), commemorated the rededication of the Temple by Judas Maccabeus after his victory over the tyrant Antiochus IV Epiphanes in 165 B.C. Purim, a more secular observance celebrated on the fourteenth and fifteenth of Adar (February-March), commemorated the victory of the Jews in Persia through the leadership of Esther and Mordecai (Est 9:31).

Part III

How to Study and
Pray the Bible

ELEVEN

Personal Bible Study

Reading about the Bible is dangerous. The project can become so absorbing that we never get to the point of reading the Bible itself. Energy is consumed in introduction and preparation: books, articles, commentaries—all of them fascinating, but none of them the inspired word of God. But direct involvement with God's word is the goal, not an endless circling around it. This Bible study handbook may be dangerous to your spiritual health. Make sure that it serves as a doorway to the Bible and not as a substitute for it.

Bible reading is not difficult. The difficulty lies in making time for Bible reading and then actually beginning to do it. That first step is the most important and often the most difficult. Once Bible reading becomes a priority, the sky's the limit. Choices arise about which book to read first, which tools and aids to use—but there is no end to the helps available. Though direct reading of the Bible may always produce spiritual profit, the principle behind this chapter (and underlying the book) is that preparation and study enhance the impact of the biblical word in our lives. Bible study may take place privately or in company with others. This present chapter concentrates on norms and programs for individual study, the next on plans for group study. Group study, of course, incorporates the same norms and ordinarily is accompanied by personal private study of the Bible.

Many people have begun programs of personal Bible study at one time or another and then found that their good intention has slowly drifted away. Above I stated that the first step, setting aside a time for Bible study and establishing it as a priority, is most important. Without that, the program never gets off the ground. But once study is underway there are some further steps needed to keep it going. The key words are prayer, stability, and guidance.

Prayer keeps the study directed toward its true goal: union with God which brings healing, peace, and personal transformation. The Holy Spirit protects the study from wandering into harmful areas, and awakens one's taste for richer spiritual food.

By stability I mean that it is important to develop a realistic schedule of study to which one can be faithful on a daily or, at the least, a weekly basis. It may take some searching to find the best time of the day and the best place for this quiet time with the Lord and his inspired word. A haphazard schedule has been the downfall of many good intentions.

The Bible is a large volume and can be intimidating. Where do I begin? Do I simply plunge into this ocean? Some readers have waded into Genesis, stubbed their toe on Leviticus, and drowned in Numbers. Guidance is needed for the decision about where to begin and how to proceed. If there is no personal help available, as in a class or a group study, the individual should select appropriate study aids from the many now on the market. Several of these are listed at the end of this and following chapters.

Approaching the Word

The principles governing Catholic reading and study of the Bible are elaborated in chapters 1 and 2. The Bible is not just any book; it is the inspired word of God, which makes the presence and power of God available to the reader approaching it in faith. The first step in Bible study is prayer for guidance in listening to the divine message. Without this step, Bible study may become distorted into a mere academic exercise.

But the Bible also contains a human word, and the opposite kind of distortion is likely if the Bible's human origins and qualities are not kept constantly in mind. God did not wipe out our human nature when we received the Holy Spirit, and he did not erase the human dimension of the word given to us through the inspired writers. The methods used to discover the meaning of any human writing must be applied to the Bible as well. The first step in this process is to determine the literary form of the book or passage. As mentioned earlier, a gospel is not a psalm, and a religious statement is not necessarily a statement of historical or biological fact. The Bible contains many types of writing: biography, poetry, sermon, prophecy, apocalypse, lamentation, novella, to name a few. Without this first step of discerning the literary form, the interpreter is at the mercy of speculation and imagination. The fable of the trees (Jgs 9:8-15) becomes a historical problem, and figures of speech—like "he laughed his head off"—become causes of biological, moral, or theological dispute.

Studying a Bible Passage

Because the Bible includes various types of writing, no single method of approach will apply to every passage in the Old and New Testaments. As patterns for study, I will present plans for two types of biblical text, one from the New Testament (a Gospel passage) and one from the Old Testament (a psalm).

A Gospel Story. The five-step pattern outlined here is applicable to many biblical passages. It is a handy tool for the beginning Bible reader or for one who has advanced training in Scripture. I will explain the five steps and then illustrate their use with a Gospel story.

Step 1. *Simply read the passage straight through.*

Step 2. *Read the passage again slowly, marking down anything that needs special attention or any questions that come to mind.* This could include words you don't fully understand, names you might not be familiar with, ideas that seem central to the passage, and events that are referred to.

Step 3. *Answer the questions as well as you can by looking at the context of the passage* in the particular Gospel. The cross-references in your Bible will be a great help here.

Step 4. *Seek additional information* and insights from a Bible commentary or other Bible study aid.

Step 5. *Listen for the particular personal message God offers you* in this story.

As an example for applying these steps, we will use Luke 7:18-23, a story involving Jesus and John the Baptist.

Step 1. *Read the passage.* Luke 7:18-23 appears in the New American Bible as follows:

The disciples of John told him about all these things. John summoned two of his disciples and sent them to the Lord to ask, "Are you the one who is to come, or should we look for another?" When the men came to him, they said, "John the Baptist has sent us to you to ask, 'Are you the one who is to come, or should we look for another?'" At that time he cured many of their diseases, sufferings, and evil spirits; he also granted sight to many who were blind. And he said to them in reply, "Go and tell John what you have seen and heard: the blind regain their sight, the lame walk, lepers are cleansed, the deaf hear, the dead are raised, the poor have the good news proclaimed to them. And blessed is the one who takes no offense at me."

Step 2. *Read and ask questions.* For example: Where is John at this time? Why doesn't he ask Jesus these questions himself? Why does John, the forerunner of the Messiah, seem to doubt Jesus' identity? How will the actions Jesus mentions provide an answer to John? What does the final sentence mean?

Step 3. *Look at the context.* This step and the next may expand almost limitlessly to meet the needs and interests of each reader. By looking back to see what the Gospel of Luke has already told us about John the Baptist, we learn that John is confined in prison (see Luke 3:19-20). That explains why he cannot approach Jesus directly with his questions. Elsewhere in Luke's Gospel we find additional information about John. He was introduced as one who would go before the Lord "in the spirit and power of Elijah" (1:17). His father echoed this by calling him a prophet and forerunner (1:76). Examples of John's preaching are given, along with his own message about the Messiah to come and the nature of the Messiah's ministry

(3:3-18). From these we learn that John has been preaching words of punishment in unquenchable fire and expecting a Messiah who will speak in harsh denunciation of sinners (3:17).

Verses 18 and 19 of our passage mention that John sent his disciples to Jesus after they had told him of "all these things." The most recent happenings reported are Jesus' teaching on love of enemies, divine compassion, and building a solid spiritual foundation (6:27-49), his curing of the centurion's son, and his raising of the widow's son (7:1-17). With these things in mind, we begin to answer our questions about why John seemed uncertain of Jesus' identity. Jesus is not fulfilling the pattern of fierce warning and strict reproof that John had foretold. John wonders whether he has made a mistake in proclaiming that Jesus is the one who is to come. In his response to John, Jesus calls attention to his works of mercy for the blind, the crippled, lepers, and the poor. His final sentence is the punch line: "Blessed is the one who takes no offense at me." This beatitude implies that John was mistaken, not in his identification of Jesus as the "one who is to come," but in his understanding of Jesus' mission. John must take Jesus as he is, correcting his expectation to fit the reality. Jesus is not the harsh prophet John was called to be. If John holds on to his mistaken notions about Jesus, he will not be able to see that Jesus is truly God's Messiah. Jesus will instead become a scandal or stumbling block for him.

Step 4. *Consult commentaries and other study aids.* As an example, I will consult three commentaries on the Gospel of Luke. The first is Eugene Laverdiere's *Luke* (Liturgical Press, 1982) in the New Testament Message series. Fr. LaVerdiere is known for his work in making the biblical word accessible to lay and religious groups. He helps the reader understand a biblical passage in its original context and to see its relevance for Christian life in the world of today.

In my pamphlet in the *Collegeville Bible Commentary* (Liturgical Press, 1983), I call attention to some Old Testament passages underlying the account and also make the point that verse 23 contains a challenge not only to John but to anyone confronted by Jesus: do not let your preconceived notion of Jesus be a stumbling block to you.

The scholarly commentary by Joseph A. Fitzmyer, S.J., in the *Anchor Bible* (Doubleday, 1981), compares the passage in Luke's Gospel to the account of the same episode in Matthew's Gospel. Both are said to come from an earlier source known as Q (from *Quelle*, the German word for "source").

Step 5. *Listen to God's personal word to you.* This listening for God's personal word in a spirit of prayer and obedience is the goal of true Bible study. A genuine challenge to our heart will lead toward greater conversion of life. It will not be a mere intellectual exercise but will awaken virtue and call us into action. One reader confronted with this passage may feel a kinship with John in prison because of a particular loneliness, a difficulty in making sense of life's twists and turns, or a feeling of separation from God. Even in prison John reached out to others through his disciples; he remained faithful to his own mission till death. Another reader may need to be reminded of the Christian mission of making Jesus present in service to the sick, the poor, and the outcast. Still another may be struck by the challenge of verse 23, realizing that a false expectation or understanding of Jesus has been a stumbling block. This may lead to a reassessment of prayer and of one's awareness of the presence of Jesus in others.

Studying a Psalm

The personal study of Old Testament books requires some adjustments for a Christian. These books cannot be treated simply the same way as the New Testament books that breathe faith in Jesus Christ. The psalms are not the only type of literature in the Hebrew Bible any more than the Gospels are the only kind of Christian Scriptures, but the Book of Psalms seems to be a good choice to use as a pattern because the psalms were used by the New Testament writers and have remained important to Christian prayer through the centuries.

The study format contains eight steps: first the reading of the psalm, then three steps devoted to the meaning of the psalm as an expression of Old Testament Hebrew faith, three devoted to the Christian application and use of the psalm in prayer, and finally, another reading of the psalm.

Step 1. *Read the psalm through,* preferably aloud, in order to appreciate its poetic flavor.

Step 2. *Summarize the meaning of the psalm in one or two sentences.* It is impossible to encompass everything, but this helps grasp the main thrust of the psalm as the Hebrew author conceived it.

Step 3. *Study the psalm with the help of footnotes, commentary, other aids.* This phase will investigate the circumstances of the psalm's composition, the poetic structure, references to people and events, the meaning of obscure names and terms. This step is essential for understanding the psalm in its original context of Jewish faith.

Step 4. *Relate thoughts in the psalm to central themes of Hebrew faith,* themes such as salvation, creation, exodus, covenant, messiah, king, sin, longing for God. References to related Old Testament passages can be located with the help of a concordance or a Bible dictionary.

Step 5. *Seek a Christian meaning.* With this step the Christian reading of the psalm begins. Up to now the study has concerned itself only with the psalm as a production of Hebrew faith by a Hebrew poet. The present step goes beyond the literal meaning of the psalm. It seeks consciously for a Christian meaning to give expression to Christian faith. Perhaps Christ is speaking in the psalm, or he may be the one spoken about. The Christian reader may be the speaker or the one spoken about, or it may be the Church as a whole.

Step 6. *Relate thoughts in the psalm to themes of Christian salvation.* This is the New Testament version of step 4 and will complete some of the themes discovered there, for example: new creation, new exodus, new covenant. The student searches for New Testament texts as expanded references to the psalm's ideas, phrases, and words. The purpose here is to deepen the Christian penetration of the psalm so that Christian images will come alive when the psalm is used in prayer.

The Christian reader is free to let mind and memory play over these connections, not worrying that some associations might not be rooted in the text. At this point the psalm study is no longer an exercise in interpretation. The literal meaning of the text has already been secured in step 3 of this study. Now the Christian reader gives spiritual imagination free rein to enliven the ancient words with personal faith.

Step 7. *Compose a prayer using the phraseology of the psalm and reflecting personal faith.* Psalm-prayers are part of the Church's liturgical tradition. They have been revived recently as summarizing prayers at the end of psalms in the Liturgy of the Hours.

Step 8. *Read the psalm straight through again*, prayerfully, enjoying the new resonance as a result of your study.

To illustrate the use of this eight-step method I have selected Psalm 110, a psalm which may be more familiar than others since it is one of the few quoted directly in the New Testament.

Step 1. *Read the psalm.* Psalm 110 appears in the New American Bible as follows:

The Lord says to you my lord:
    "Take your throne at my right hand,
    while I make your enemies your footstool."
The scepter of your sovereign might
    the Lord will extend from Zion.
The Lord says: "Rule over your enemies!
    Yours is princely power from the day of your birth.
In holy splendor before the daystar,
    like the dew I begot you."
The Lord has sworn and will not waver:
    "Like Melchizedek you are a priest forever."
At your right hand is the Lord,
    who crushes kings on the day of wrath.
Who, robed in splendor, judges nations,
    crushes heads across the wide earth,
    Who drinks from the brook by the wayside
and thus holds high his head.

Step 2. *Summarize the psalm:* God appoints the king and gives him a share in the divine authority over Israel. God will protect the king and his successors and will aid him in struggles with the enemies of Israel.

Step 3. *Literary investigation.* Psalm 110 belongs to the group of royal psalms, those which were originally prayers for the kings at the time of enthronement or prayers of thanksgiving and praise because of victory. These frequently became praises of God's kingship over Israel or over all creation. Psalm 110 was later used with reference to the Messiah, that is, it was understood as foreshadowing the mission of the Messiah or Anointed One to come. The psalm was composed during the time of the monarchy (from King David until the Babylonian Exile, 1000-587 B.C.). The title "A psalm of David" above the text does not necessarily mean that David wrote it. The title was added later and may mean only that it belongs with the psalms that exalt the Davidic kingship.

Verse 1: The Lord God speaks to my lord the king. The place of honor is at the right: this implies that the king participates in God's rule. A victorious king would sometimes place his foot on the neck of a defeated enemy (Jos 10:24).

Verse 2: The master of ceremonies for the enthronement seems to be the speaker. The statement about the scepter reiterates that the king exercises the Lord's authority.

Verse 3: The day of accession to the throne is spoken of as the day of the king's birth. The references to "before the daystar ... I begot you" is probably a statement of belief in God's power over the rulers of darkness as well as his control of the day. Contemporary pagan lore assigned the day and the night to different sets of gods.

Verse 4: Melchizedek was the king of Jerusalem and priest of God under the title El Elyon ("God Most High") during the time of Abraham (Gn 14:18). The king is invested with a priestly as well as a kingly role, which is unusual.

Verse 5: Now God is at the king's right hand, to indicate that the power of God is at the king's disposal. The "day of wrath" is probably a reference to the Day of the Lord mentioned by the prophets, the time when the enemies of God and of his people will be punished.

Verse 6: This is an expansion with vivid imagery of the idea in the preceding verse.

Verse 7: The drink by the wayside either refers to refreshment during battle or to the customary drink of the king from the spring of Gihon during the royal ritual. In the latter sense the water is a source of power helping the king conquer his enemies.

Step 4. *Old Testament themes:* God's kingship, central to the psalm, has many references, for instance: "The Lord is king; let the earth rejoice" (Ps 97:1; see Ps 2:6, 98:9). The story of Melchizedek is in Genesis 14:18-20. The Day of the Lord: "I ... announce vindication, I who am mighty to save" (Is 63:1; see Amos 5:18; Joel 2:1). Water: "Wherever this water comes the sea shall be made fresh" (Ez 47:9; see Gn 2:6). Other themes are Mount Zion (verse 2), God's personal creation and call (verse 3).

Step 5. *Christian reading of the psalm:* a Christian may hear God the Father speaking to Jesus, giving him kingly dominion and priestly office as his only-begotten son. Each Christian participates in the kingship and priesthood of Christ, so the psalm may be read as a personal promise of the Father's protection and guidance.

Step 6. *New Testament themes:* Some Christian themes are Jesus' kingship, his priesthood according to the order of Melchizedek, his preexistence as the Word of God, and the living water. In connection with this psalm there are direct quotes in the New Testament (for example, Mt 22:44; Hb 1:13) and some allusions to guide one's search for echoing texts.

Step 7. *Psalm prayer:* "God our Father, you gave us your Son to be our king and priest. May we by your grace remain faithful heirs to his kingdom and, by our own share in his priesthood, offer the sacrifice of praise that gives you praise forever and ever."

Step 8. *Read the psalm again,* aloud, prayerfully.

Aids for Private Bible Study

The resources for personal Bible study listed below have been updated from the first edition. Those arranged also for use in group study are marked with an asterisk (*); those especially helpful for prayer are marked with two asterisks (**). Other resources for private Bible study are listed among the aids for group Bible study and for scriptural prayer in the two following chapters. The listing of the sources below and in the other bibliographies is not meant to be a general recommendation of all the materials mentioned; the names and descriptions are provided for the reader's information. Phone numbers and websites of publishers are in Appendix 2.

**John F. Craghan, C.SS.R., *Psalms for All Seasons* (Liturgical Press). Shows how the Psalms may be used according to the various moods and needs of life.

Credence Cassettes. A lengthy catalog of taped lectures on themes, sections, and individual books by prominent Scripture scholars.

Gillian Crow, *Grains of Salt and Rays of Light: Reflections on St. Matthew's Gospel* (Alba House). Points the reader toward the application of Matthew's Gospel to everyday life in the modern world.

**God's Word Today*. A monthly magazine which provides a daily guide for reading the Bible, focusing on one book or theme each month. The editor is Stephen Binz.

Joseph A. Grassi, *The Spiritual Message of the New Testament* (Alba House Communications). Thirty-four audio cassettes in nine volumes cover all the books of the New Testament.

Marilyn Gustin, *Discovering the Spirit of the Gospels* (Liguori).

Daniel Harrington, S.J., *How to Read the Gospels* (New City Press, 1996).

Journeys into ... (St. Anthony Messenger Press). One volume for each gospel. Workbooks providing tools for digging into the Gospels, exploring their meaning, and considering their application to one's life.

Oscar Lukefahr, C.M., *A Catholic Guide to the Bible* (Liguori, revised edition), book with workbook.

George Martin, *Reading Scripture As the Word of God: Practical Approaches and Attitudes* (Servant Books, 4th edition, 1999), 224 pages. This book is an excellent first introduction to studying and praying the Bible. The author is noted for his skill in presenting sound knowledge in clear language.

Rea McDonnell, S.S.N.D., *When God Comes Close: A Journey Through Scripture* (Pauline Books and Media), 172 pages.

Richard T.A. Murphy, O.P., *Introduction to the Prophets of Israel* (Pauline Books and Media), 123 pages.

Mary Reed Newland, *A Popular Guide through the Old Testament* (St. Mary's Press, 1999), 280 pages.

Kevin O'Sullivan, *Living Parables* (Franciscan Press), 120 pages. Shows the spiritual application of some thirty gospel parables to our times.

William Peatman, *The Beginning of the Gospel: Mark's Story of Jesus* (Liturgical Press), 61 pages. Helps the reader share the wonder and thrill of the first disciples in meeting Jesus.

Patricia Datchuck Sánchez, *Formed in the Word* (Sheed and Ward), 228 pages. An aid for pondering the challenges of Scripture for life today.

Karl A. Schultz, The Bible for Dummies (IDG Books).

Share the Word (Paulist Catholic Evangelization Center). A magazine providing background and reflections on the daily lectionary readings (the Scripture passages read at Mass). The material aims to help readers grow in their relationship with Christ through Scripture and become evangelizing disciples. The editor is Anthony Bosnick. An introductory one-year subscription (seven issues) is $15.00.

Spiritual Commentaries (New City Press). A series of book-length commentaries on books and groups of books in the Bible by noted scholars, written at an introductory level to help readers grasp the messages of the biblical texts.

**The Word Among Us*. A magazine of meditations and prayer starters based on the daily lectionary readings, with other articles on spiritual themes, personal testimonies, and book reviews. The editor is Leo Zanchettin. Eleven issues a year, $20.00 per year.

TWELVE

Group Bible Study

Many people find it easier or more profitable to do some or all of their Bible study in a group rather than privately. Groups offer the support and enthusiasm of other members and the stimulus of others' ideas, a sense of guidance and direction, and an opportunity to share prayer. Many of the aids for private Bible study are designed for group use as well. Most programs combine the homework of private study with meetings for discussion of the selected passages.

Bible study groups will vary in their focus depending on the background and interest of the members. Members of an academic community may emphasize the historical and doctrinal areas and depend much on scholarly, critical methods and resources. A group focusing on prayer and reflection might be interested solely in the present implications of the word in the lives of the participants. Most of the aids listed at the end of this and the preceding chapter are directed somewhere in between these extremes. They are planned for a cross-section of people who seek to deepen their knowledge of the faith (doctrinally and historically) while also making personal application of the message. The materials usually permit a greater or lesser use of scholarly methods and sources. A great service to parishes and adult education coordinators since the first edition of this book is the survey of Catholic Bible study programs by Sister Macrina

Scott, O.S.F., director of the Catholic Biblical School of the Archdiocese of Denver. She reviewed 150 individual programs and 17 series in *Picking the "Right" Bible Study Program: Reviews of 150 Recommended Programs With a Listing of the Top 15* (see bibliography).

The following pages will describe some of the methods of group Bible study, and the bibliography at the end of the chapter will provide leads for further information about particular programs. Experience has shown the importance of a number of elements for a fruitful group Bible study.

1. *Prayer.* The personal study and the group sessions must be conducted in a context of prayer. Without this, Bible study can dissolve into just another intellectual exercise. It will soon lose its power for furthering the spiritual growth of the participants.

2. *Homework.* Participants must dedicate themselves to Bible reading and study between the group sessions, preferably daily. The word "homework" is used loosely; study is implied but in the context of a daily "quiet time" in which the biblical word may find its own depths in the heart of the believer.

3. *Training of Discussion Leaders.* Bible discussion leaders are ordinarily not Scripture experts, nor do they need to be. Their function is to facilitate and coordinate the group search for meaning and inspiration in the word of God. Untrained leaders can fall into the role of answerers, defenders of the faith, or teachers, or they may permit monopolies or quarrels. Under such conditions, the most willing participants are driven away.

4. *Strict Meeting Schedule.* Participants have a right to know how much time they are investing at a group meeting. The meeting must be kept within strict time limits so that all may plan for other commitments, baby-sitters, transportation, and so forth. The enthusiasm of particular members may be given

free rein after the scheduled meeting in a coffee-and-cookies setting.

Additional ingredients such as a program for children simultaneous to the group meeting will be helpful in some situations. But if any of the four elements itemized above are missing or allowed to diminish in importance, absenteeism will increase. Without prayer or homework the sense of personal growth or divine communion will fade; without good leaders and a strict schedule, the group will appear to be out of control.

Lecture and Discussion

A favored approach for many programs of adult faith formation in the Church is the lecture followed by questioning or by discussion in groups. But until recently, smaller Catholic communities were at a disadvantage because of the scarcity of trained lecturers. Advances in electronics have made experts widely available on video and audio recordings. Catholic Scripture lecture series have been developed for most of the Bible and made available through Liturgical Press, Paulist Press, Alba House, Credence Cassettes, and other publishers. Brief descriptions appear in the bibliographies, and addresses are provided in Appendix 2 for further information.

Sunday Readings

Many parishes arrange for group reflection and sharing on the readings of the approaching Sunday. Sometimes this is part of a process of homily development, the priests and deacons of the parish sharing with one another, with the parish staff, or with a wider selection of people as they prepare to bring the word to their congregation. This process is described in the instruction of the U.S. Bishops, *Fulfilled in Your Hearing*.

But the discussion of the Sunday readings is more commonly the sharing of a group of lay Catholics which may take place in a private home or may be part of a more structured adult faith formation program between Masses on Sunday morning. A helpful periodical for this kind of discussion is *Share the Word* from the Paulists.

Sharing the Story

The importances of storytelling has been emphasized recently in theology and religious education. Religious truths may be communicated through concepts, as they have been for generations in catechisms and theological monographs, but stories of faith are a much older form with a simple attractiveness and power. Writers like Fathers John Dunne and John Shea point to the narrative techniques of the biblical writers and to Jesus' penchant for teaching in parables. We come to understand our own personal story by plumbing the stories of those who have lived before us.

Sharing the stories of the Bible, among which for Christians the Gospel stories take pride of place, is not, strictly speaking, Bible study. Group leaders should do preliminary study in order to protect the study group from straying onto tangents or falling into false interpretations.

In some groups, sharing of biblical stories takes the following format. After an opening prayer or hymn, the leader gives a general introduction to the passage selected and the reasons for having chosen it. The passage is read, and then members are asked to respond, one by one, to an opening question. For example, with the story of the call of the first disciples, the question might be, "Is there anyone you know for whom you would drop everything?" The individual responses are not discussed but simply stated.

After this, the passage is read aloud again. The leader now begins the discussion, using questions to help participants apply the biblical passage to their own lives. The session proceeds for the allotted time, ending with prayer. The attractiveness of this method is its provision for immediate personal involvement in the biblical stories of salvation with or without preliminary study.

Continuing Studies Series

In this classification are ongoing Scripture study programs which cover the Bible book by book or section by section over a long period of time. Some books and tapes are designed as introductions to the Bible or surveys of the Old and New Testaments, or as studies of particular biblical writings, as for example in a parish Lenten program for adult faith formation. But here we are looking at programs designed for longer study.

Some of the cassette offerings mentioned under the heading "Lecture and Discussion" are usable by either individuals or groups, and either individually or in a series. Good leadership can combine the single tapes into a comprehensive and vital ongoing Bible study program. Programs designed as long-term comprehensive series for the study of the Bible by adult

Catholics have been rare. But one of them, the *Little Rock Scripture Study,* has expanded in recent years. And a new popular Bible study for Catholic adults has been published by Paulist Press.

Little Rock Scripture Study

Little Rock Scripture Study, which observed its twenty-fifth anniversary in 1999, is a parish-based Bible study for adults (English and Spanish) and for young adults. It involves daily personal study (using a study guide and commentary), small-group faith-sharing, wrap-up lectures (with a local speaker or on video or audio tape), and group prayer. Most of the materials study entire books of the Bible, though there are some thematic studies, as well as four video-based studies. The average length of a study is ten weeks.

The appeal of the Little Rock program beyond Arkansas seems to be based on the following factors: it was designed for a diocese of ample territory and few Catholics, with a scarcity of priests and religious, and possessing no Catholic seminary or institution of higher learning. Lay leadership is basic, no experts are needed for the local meetings, and there is a strong emphasis on prayer.

Study materials provided in this program include a Catholic commentary (any Catholic commentary is usable by individuals but the Liturgical Press pamphlets in the Collegeville Bible Commentary are included), a booklet containing questions on the biblical text for daily home study, and video or audio lectures on the unit under study. The selection and training of group discussion leaders is considered essential to the program;

a booklet and tapes providing material for local training are sent as the first mailing.

The first few Foundation studies follow a careful sequence as a parish group becomes familiar with the approach to biblical material. The opening study covers the Acts of the Apostles, selected because of its story of the emerging Church and the immediate applicability of the issues to the home and parish life of the participants. After this come studies of one of the four Gospels, Paul's captivity letters (Philippians, Philemon, Colossians, Ephesians), and the Book of Exodus.

Some parishes prefer to preface the study of the biblical books with one or more of the four video-based introductory programs: Introduction to the Bible, Overview of Old Testament, Overview of New Testament, and Lands of the Bible.

Other courses include studies of all the books of the New Testament, either separately if large (1 Corinthians) or in groups if small (James, 1 and 2 Peter, Jude). Besides Exodus, mentioned above, studies are available for twelve other Old Testament books. There are also thematic studies on the Infancy Narratives, the Passion and Resurrection Narratives, and Women in the Old Testament.

The first lesson of the study of the Acts of the Apostles gives an idea of the general approach. This lesson covers the first two chapters of Acts. The question booklet contains eighteen questions for home study for each week of the series—three questions each for six days of study. Some of the questions are informational: "What period of time is dealt with in this biblical book?" Others are doctrinal: "What does it mean to be 'baptized with the Holy Spirit'?" (Acts 1:5). This question is accompanied with biblical cross-references (Lk 3:16; Acts 2:38;

Rom 5:5; Eph 1:13), and the commentary is available for further research. Still other questions are personal: "The disciples spent the time of waiting for the Holy Spirit in prayer. What are your best times for prayer?" Participants write their responses to bring to the group discussion at the weekly meeting.

On the night of the weekly meeting, leaders meet from 6:30 to 7:20 P.M. for prayer and discussion of the questions in preparation for leading their groups. Other participants arrive by seven-thirty. The meeting begins with a song and opening prayer, then the gathering breaks into groups of ten to fifteen members for a fifty-minute discussion. All reconvene in the assembly room for the lecture at eight-thirty. This may be given by a local participant or a guest speaker, or a video or audio cassette may be used. The session ends with prayer at nine o'clock.

Group leaders are instructed that the main goal of their Scripture discussion is "to listen together to the Word of God in the Bible chapters under study and to help the participants realize its meaning and challenge for their lives." Some minutes are spent in conversational prayer. Not all questions are covered every time, but those which the leader has selected as most important and helpful to the group.

Paulist Program

The Paulist Bible Study Program consists of eight units. In the Old Testament, there are *Israel Becomes a People,* which serves as an introduction to the study of the Old Testament and covers the books of Genesis and Exodus; *Prophets and Kings; Out of Exile;* and *Isaiah: Message and Vision.* The New Testament units are *Jesus and the Gospels; Paul, Missionary to the Gentiles;*

John's Message; and *Galatians and Romans.*

Participants each have a workbook and prepare for the weekly meeting by reading appointed Bible passages in a time of prayer, studying assigned sections from a companion text (*Reading the Old Testament,* by Lawrence Boadt, C.S.P., or *Reading the New Testament,* by Pheme Perkins), and reading in the workbook focus materials for the coming group meeting.

The weekly group meeting is designed to last two hours. This consists of an opening prayer (5 minutes), a review of contents, with opportunity for discussion and questions (25 minutes), a video on the material (20 minutes), a learning activity (25 minutes), faith sharing, based on principles and techniques of the RENEW program (25 minutes), and a closing prayer (10 minutes).

A leader's manual provides detailed instruction for the group leader. It contains all the material contained in the participant's workbook plus background information which is helpful for guiding the discussion of the review questions and the learning activity. In addition to the companion texts used by all participants, the manual points leaders to readings in other sources to flesh out the information.

An example of the method of this series is unit 4 in *Jesus and the Gospels* entitled "The Resurrection of Jesus." In preparation for the weekly meeting, participants privately read the appropriate chapter from the Perkins text and the account of the resurrection appearances in the four Gospels. They are also asked to reflect on the Focus statement and the Review of Contents questions which will be discussed by the group.

The opening prayer includes a time of preparation with music and silence, a gathering prayer by the leader, and a song. The Review of Contents concentrates on the variants in Matthew 28 and Luke 24. The leader's manual contains a chart of the narratives of the Empty Tomb and guidance for responses to the discussion questions.

A video deals with the Resurrection and the meaning it had for disciples grounded in the Jewish tradition. The participant's workbook contains a series of questions to focus attention on the issues dealt with in the video.

After the break, the learning activity encourages participants to share their reflections on the Gospel narratives, including what they have written before the meeting and in response to the video. The leader's manual gives more extensive guidance for this segment.

A time of faith sharing personalizes the message of the resurrection narratives. The Emmaus event in Luke 24 is read by the group in segments, with opportunity to summarize in one word what each passage means personally to the participants. Additional reflection questions are available in case time is available, for instance: "What keeps you from recognizing Jesus 'on the way'?"

The closing prayer centers on the Resurrection, with a "Call to Remember" using Paul's witness in 1 Corinthians 15, and a Litany of New Testament verses on the Resurrection, accompanied by the breaking and distribution of bread in light of the Emmaus story in Luke 15. The weekly meeting ends with a closing song.

The follow-up for home study has two parts: journaling on the just completed lesson with help from directions and questions in the workbook, and readings from four sources (Anthony Morelli, *Understanding the Gospels;* Raymond E. Brown, S.S., *Responses to 101 Questions on the Bible; The Catholic Study Bible;* and Hammond's *Atlas of the Bible Lands*).

Aids for Group Bible Study

The resources listed below are current materials arranged for group Bible study. Those arranged also for use in private study are marked with three asterisks (***); those especially helpful for prayer are marked with two asterisks (**). Other resources for group Bible study are listed among the aids for private Bible study in the preceding chapter and among the aids for scriptural prayer in the following chapter. Addresses of publishers are in Appendix 2.

***Etienne Charpentier, *How to Read the Old Testament* and *How to Read the New Testament* (Crossroad). Basic introductions with maps, charts, and drawings, arranged for individual or group study. Facilitator and participant guides are also available.

Mitch Finley, *Living Scripture* (Sheed and Ward). These are reproducible lectionary-based reflections on the Sunday Scripture readings, suitable for small-group reflection and discussion. The emphasis is on the message of the biblical texts for day-to-day spirituality.

Barbara J. Fleischer, *Facilitating for Growth: A Guide for Scripture Study Groups and Small Christian Communities* (Liturgical Press), 160 pages. How to develop great small-group facilitators.

Little Rock Scripture Study Program. An extensive and well-developed program of materials for parish group Bible study. Packets focusing on selected biblical books include video and audio tape lectures and question booklets for home study and group discussion. Accompanied by Liturgical Press pamphlet commentaries. Leadership training packet provided for essential preparation.

***Alfred McBride, O.Praem., Our Sunday Visitor's Popular Bible Study (Our Sunday Visitor Press). Series of books on the Gospels, Acts, and Revelation, providing commentary, with questions. There is also a director's guide.

Paulist Bible Study Program (Paulist Press). Videotapes and printed materials for leaders and participants provide an in-depth, extensive introduction to the whole Bible.

***Kevin Perrotta, *Six Weeks With the Bible* (Loyola Press, 2000). Books are either eighty or ninety-six pages. Booklets for group Bible discussion, providing background resources, numerous questions, suggestions for prayer, and excerpts from Christian tradition. Each volume explores a book or portions of a book of the Bible in six sessions.

Kevin Perrotta, *Your One-Stop Guide to the Bible* (Servant Publications). An excellent basic introduction to reading the Bible.

***Margaret Nutting Ralph, *Discovering* ... (Paulist Press). Three volumes: Genesis, Exodus, Samuel; Isaiah, Job, Proverbs, Psalms; Acts, Paul's letters, Revelation. Introductions to the biblical books, with numerous questions. Designed for high school instruction, but could also work for adult study groups.

***Macrina Scott, O.S.F., *Bible Stories Revisited* (St. Anthony Messenger Press). Encourages individuals and groups to read the Bible through the lens of their own life stories. Especially valuable for older readers.

Macrina Scott, O.S.F., *Picking the "Right" Bible Study Program* (ACTA Publications, revised edition). A detailed, systematic review of Catholic and Protestant group Bible study materials, with recommendations for Catholic users.

Karen Sue Smith and Donna L. Ciangio, *"Til the Lord Comes ..."* (St. Anthony Messenger Press). Six lectionary-based reflections for small-group discussion.

Sunday by Sunday (Good Ground Press). A short, weekly, lectionary-based guide to exploring and praying Scripture in group settings. Published by Sisters of St. Joseph of Carondelet.

***Gerard Weber and Robert Miller, *Breaking Open the Gospel of* ... (St. Anthony Messenger Press). One volume on each Gospel. Commentary invites the reader into personal encounter with Jesus; an abundance of questions suitable for individual and group use.

Who Do You Say That I Am? (Alba House). An exploration of the contemporary relevance of the Synoptic Gospels designed for use by small groups.

THIRTEEN

Bible Prayer

Bible study is not for the accumulation of information about a book. This holy book is written in faith. And only a person of faith, one open to the Bible as God's word, can read it with understanding. The words do not speak to the mind only, but to the heart. They create a relationship with the divine Author. Therefore all authentic Bible study leads to prayer.

The sacred Scriptures are a privileged channel of God's revelation. Vatican Council II reformulated the Catholic teaching that revelation is twofold: God's gift of himself to us and the communication of truth about himself and his plan for our salvation: "In his goodness and wisdom, God chose to reveal himself and to make known to us the hidden purpose of his will.... Through divine revelation, God chose to show forth and communicate himself and the eternal decisions of his will regarding the salvation of mankind" (*Constitution on Divine Revelation*, sections 2 and 6). Primary and essential to revelation is God's communication of himself, a personal gift to his children; and essential to our receiving revelation is a personal loving response in faith. An understanding of the body of authentic doctrine about God, revelation in the second sense, enhances this essential response but cannot replace it.

Wherever revelation is authentically transmitted, both God and his saving truth are presented together. This is the way the

Bible is made available in the Church. God gives himself. "In the sacred books, the Father who is in heaven meets his children with great love and speaks with them" (*Constitution on Divine Revelation,* section 21). The truth about God is learned and preached: "The Sacred Scriptures contain the word of God and, since they are inspired, really are the word of God; and so the study of the sacred page is, as it were, the soul of sacred theology" (section 24). The Bible is a library but also a temple, and must be opened in a spirit of worship: "Let the faithful remember that prayer should accompany the reading of Sacred Scripture, so that God and his people may talk together; for, in the words of St. Ambrose, 'we speak to him when we pray; we hear him when we read the divine words'" (section 25).

This attitude of the Church on the prayerful use of the Bible is enshrined in the public liturgy. The formularies for the Mass and the sacraments are inspired by Scripture texts. The Liturgy of the Hours is even more thoroughly an arrangement of biblical readings and psalms. This Divine Office, whether in the complete form or one of the abridged editions, is for many people the best introduction to scriptural prayer. This chapter will be concerned, though, with other ways to use the Bible for personal prayer. While methods are described for private use, they often lend themselves well to group prayer, as in several of the Bible study programs indicated earlier.

Lectio Divina

This Latin phrase often pops up in writings on spirituality. It is left in Latin not because it is untranslatable but because it refers to an ancient Christian approach to biblical prayer which is not captured in a single English phrase. Literally, *lectio divina* means "divine reading," though "holy reading" is a more common translation and "prayerful reading" is closer to the mark. It might even be translated by the familiar "spiritual reading," though this modern term often implies reading for information or insight about the spiritual life. *Lectio divina* is a search for union, not for knowledge; for transformation, not information about the spiritual life. It stresses the processes of reading the text, mulling it over, praying about it, and going beyond it in contemplation. There is also a particular type of spiritual journal in this tradition, which involves recording and weaving together biblical quotes that have powerfully affected a person's prayer life.

The most common form of *lectio divina* is unhurried reading, reflecting, and praying over a selected Bible passage. This may be the epistle or gospel of the Mass of the day or a passage chosen for other reasons. After taking time to pray and enter fully into the presence of God, the Scripture is read slowly, with particular attention paid to the inner voice of God. If some word or thought needs time for reflection or prayer, the reader stops and reflects on God's word before moving on. The reading may cover one sentence or a chapter, depending on the leading of God. There is no pressure to complete a particular text; the text is a launching pad to communion with God.

Selecting, for example, the hymn of redemption in St. Paul's Letter to the Philippians (2:6-11), a reading might proceed at this pace: "Though he was in the form of God"—reflections on Jesus' identity as God's own Son, including the recalling of his Transfiguration on the mountaintop, with moments for direct communion with Jesus either in conversation or silence. "He did not deem equality with God something to be grasped at"—memories of the stories of Jesus' humble birth, his association with outcasts of all kinds, his physical exhaustion after a day on the dusty road; thoughts of my own search for human glory, the temptations to grasp tightly the good things of this world; a prayer for release from the demon of self-centeredness. "Rather, he emptied himself and took the form of a slave"—more recollections of Jesus' self-sacrifice for others, his coming among us "not to be served but to serve"; mental pictures of slavery; thoughts of the slaveries of sin that grip people today, and my own slaveries; a resolution to serve others, especially those closest to me, in imitation of Jesus. And so the reading continues, gradually, unhurriedly, sometimes stopping indefinitely under the inspiration of grace.

One secret to success in this form of biblical prayer is to select a reading that is already familiar, usually a Gospel or an epistle. The reason for this is to guard against being driven along by the desire to know what is coming next. The goal is not increased knowledge, remember, but closer union. Even unfamiliar texts can be "tamed" for this exercise by reading sections through at the beginning of the prayer time, and then going back to the beginning for an unhurried journey through the text.

Meditation

This and the other types of biblical prayer described here may all be seen as particular phases of the general approach called *lectio divina,* but they are also distinct methods in their own right. "Meditation" is a slippery word in contemporary writing about prayer because it is used to identify two different practices. In the practice of the early Christian monks, meditation meant repeating over and over biblical verses which had been learned by heart. While their hands were busy at work they would repeat or "chew" the psalm verse or antiphon from the community prayer. The repetition of the Hail Marys in the Rosary comes from this tradition. The words have meaning, but after awhile the focus is not so much on the meaning as on the presence of God. Meditation is then the same as "contemplation," the unitive prayer beyond words.

Meditation today more commonly means reflecting on the meaning of a biblical passage, particularly with the purpose of making personal application of the word of God in one's life. This practice may lead to prayer, but it is more properly the mental exercise which precedes prayer. It is only part, for example, of the *lectio divina* method described above. If the epistle or gospel of the day's Mass is selected for meditation, the whole passage is considered as a unit. The reflection is meant to lead to personal application and resolutions. The practice known as "discursive meditation" in recent Catholic spirituality is like this. Reflection on the mysteries during the Rosary comes from this tradition.

Taking again as an example the hymn in Philippians 2:6-11, this kind of meditation views the whole passage as an insight into the humility expressed by Jesus' obedience unto death, at the heart of his work of redemption. The meditation might focus on the meaning and value of humility, with examples from the lives of Jesus and others, and with application to our own lives. Or the theme may be obedience, or suffering as the path to glory. Reflective meditation tries to plumb the mystery of these key truths, to examine them as Christian virtues, and to bring them to bear in one's own life.

Imaging

The reflection involved in "meditation" centers on ideas: the truths of revelation, spiritual insights, plans for action. Biblical "imaging" is also an activity of the mind, but with a concentration on drama, dialogue, and action rather than on concepts. The reader uses imagination to enter into the story. After reading the Gospel account of Peter's walking on the water and then faltering (Mt 14:25-33), the imagination recreates the scene: the boat rocking on the waters, the panic of the disciples when they spot Jesus, Peter's exuberant confidence and loss of nerve. The reader searches his or her own emotions in the presence of Jesus and the Twelve, and if the imagination is good enough, converses with the various participants in the drama, particularly Jesus.

The classical presentation of this method of prayer is in the *Spiritual Exercises* of St. Ignatius Loyola. Since the appearance of the Exercises in 1533, this technique of entering the Gospel stories has had a profound impact on the spiritual life of succeeding generations in the Church. But an already complicated terminology is rendered even more confusing in that St. Ignatius refers to this use of the imagination as "contemplation," which is quite different from its traditional meaning described below. It should be noted that the Exercises also incorporate other methods of prayer, such as the reflective meditation mentioned above and a "rhythmical recitation" of familiar prayers (Our Father, Hail Mary) for the deeper absorption of their meaning.

An example of St. Ignatius' method of imaging is the "contemplation" for the first day of the third week of the four-week-long Exercises. The subject is the Gospel story of Jesus' journey from Bethany to Jerusalem for the Last Supper. After a preparatory prayer, there are three preludes: a recalling of the outlines of the story (the sending of the disciples, the Passover meal, the last discourse); a mental picturing of the place (the road, the room, the table); a statement of desire for a deepening of sorrow and repentance as a result of sharing this Gospel episode.

Then come the six points of the exercise: visualizing and pondering on the persons at supper, listening to their conversation, observing their actions; then considering Jesus' willingness to suffer for us, his self-emptying humility in allowing his enemies to triumph, and the part the reader's own sins play in his suffering. The climax is the "colloquy" or conversation with Jesus, in which I share with him my own needs, hopes, questions.

This prayer of imaging is designed for Gospel stories and other narratives which have scenes and actions easily pictured in the mind. But the idea of praying a biblical text from the inside may be adapted to other types of writings. The monk John Cassian, writing in the early fifth century, found a way to "become the psalmist": "Penetrating into all the sentiments of the psalms, the monk will begin to sing them in such a way that he pours them forth with the deepest compunction of heart, not as words composed by the psalmist but as if he had written them himself as his own prayer.... Penetrating into the same state of mind in which each psalm was sung or written, we become its author, so to speak, and rather than following its meaning, we anticipate it, so that we perceive the significance of what it says even before we understand the letter" (*Conferences*, 10:11).

Contemplation

This type of prayer moves beyond the Bible to wordless and even imageless union with God, but it deserves treatment here as the goal toward which our Bible study and reading tends; and also because Christian contemplation flows from God's revelation in Jesus Christ as presented through the inspired Scriptures. It is the fourth rung of the ladder of prayer described in the Latin axiom from antiquity: *lectio, meditatio, oratio, contemplatio* (reading, meditation, prayer, contemplation).

We have come to the end of a period in our religious history when contemplative prayer was considered a preserve of the mystics and religious professionals. A layperson might hope to move into this type of prayer toward the end of life after much purification and practice. Just as the Bible has begun to come back home into the daily lives of Catholics at all levels, so is contemplative prayer being understood again as part of the spiritual heritage of every Christian. The treasured writings of contemplatives of the past are being opened up to modern believers with clear and simple instruction.

One of the principal teachers from our Western Church tradition is John Cassian, mentioned above. He urged the "poverty of a single verse" in prayer; the verse he chose was "O God, come to my assistance; O Lord, make haste to help me" (Psalm 70:2), which under his influence became the opening prayer for the Hours of the Divine Office. Other sources having new influence today are *The Cloud of Unknowing,* by an English monk of the fourteenth century, and *The Way of a Pilgrim,* in which a Russian Christian of the nineteenth century describes his search for a spiritual master who will teach him how to "pray without ceasing" (1 Thes 5:17). He is introduced to the Jesus Prayer, based on the prayer of the tax collector in the Jerusalem Temple (Lk 18:13): "Lord Jesus Christ, Son of God, have mercy on me, a sinner."

Recent instructions on contemplative prayer try to remove the mysterious aura which grew up around it. We experience this simple union with God after Communion, or in the presence of a newborn baby, or at a death, or in silent moments "doing nothing" before the Blessed Sacrament. Simple methods are being taught so that this kind of prayer may be practiced independent of the ups and downs of our moods.

Attitudes for Biblical Prayer

The chapters on individual and group Bible study have emphasized the need for prayer at the beginning of study. We are on "holy ground" (Ex 3:5) when we come into the presence of God and therefore must approach his word with reverence. How much more is this true when we pick up the Bible in order to pray, to seek communion with God. There are ways to remind ourselves of the holiness of the sacred Scriptures, to dramatize the presence and power of God in his word. The Bible may be enthroned in a room of the house with a vigil light before it, or a candle may be lit when the prayer time begins. One's prayer Bible might be kept separate from the Bible used for study, unmarked and perhaps attractively covered.

If possible, the time for prayer should be a quiet time. Silence is not always easy to arrange in a busy family; often it can be managed only at the very beginning or very end of the day. But the sounds of radio and television, chatter and noise make it difficult for the heart to listen; these interferences need to be minimized as much as possible.

If any kind of private prayer is going to have healing and sanctifying effects, it must be established on a regular basis. Regularity in brief daily periods is more valuable than long, sporadic stretches of biblical prayer. The purpose of prayer is the building of a relationship with God through his word. Like any friend, he will become better known by regular meetings, however brief, than by the chance encounter that may last hours or a day or two.

Finally, we must come to biblical prayer with an openness to be called forth like Abraham into a new country, or like Moses into a promised land. There must be a willingness to be molded and transformed under the hand of God. This means a decision to live by the word and not simply consider it an attractive philosophy. Mary is our model for scriptural prayer. She treasured the word in her heart and reflected on it (Lk 2:19), but not only that; she put it into practice (8:21).

Aids for Praying the Bible

The resources listed below are current materials arranged for biblical prayer. Those arranged also for use in private Bible study are marked with three asterisks (***); those arranged also for use in group study are marked with one asterisk (*). Other resources for biblical prayer are listed among the aids for private and group Bible study in the two preceding chapters. Addresses of publishers are in Appendix 2.

***Charlene Altemose, M.S.C., *What You Should Know about the Word of the Lord* (Liguori). Explains how we can encounter Jesus more deeply through the Liturgy of the Word in the Mass.

Christopher Aridas, *Soundings: A Thematic Guide for Daily Scripture Prayer* (Doubleday Image), 224 pages. Fr. Aridas presents 52 themes and 365 related biblical excerpts for daily prayer.

Helen Bacovcin, translator, *The Way of a Pilgrim and The Pilgrim Continues His Way* (Doubleday Image, 1978). A Russian pilgrim and the Jesus Prayer.

Jacqueline Syrup Bergan and S. Marie Schwan, *Love: A Guide to Prayer*, Take and Receive Series (Saint Mary's Press, 1985), 128 pages.

Enzio Bianchi, *Praying the Word: An Introduction to Lectio Divina* (Cistercian Publications, 1998).

Raymond E. Brown, *A Retreat With John the Evangelist* (St. Anthony Messenger Press). A noted biblical scholar creates an imaginary retreat under the guidance of the author of John's Gospel.

Walter Brueggemann, *Praying the Psalms* (Saint Mary's Press, 1993), 72 pages. How to connect the Psalms with daily life experiences.

Michael Casey, *Sacred Reading: The Ancient Art of Lectio Divina* (Triumph Books).

Christian Prayer (Catholic Book Publishing Co., 1999). One-volume edition of the Liturgy of the Hours.

Gerald Darring, *To Love and Serve* (Sheed and Ward), 84 pages. Meditations on the Sunday Scripture readings.

Daybreaks: Daily Reflections on the Readings (Liguori). A quarterly publication providing daily reflections and prayer-starters from the lectionary readings, including the responsorial psalms.

Demetrius Dumm, *Flowers in the Desert: A Spirituality of the Desert* (St. Bede's Publications, 1998).

Mary Kathleen Glavich, *The Bible Way to Prayer: God's 800 Number for Everyone* (Twenty-third Publications, 2000), 94 pages.

Thelma Hall, R.C., *Too Deep for Words: Rediscovering Lectio Divina* (Paulist Press, 1988), 110 pages. A guide to the slow, meditative, receptive mode of reading Scripture that developed in the early centuries of the Church.

William Johnston, editor, *The Cloud of Unknowing* (Doubleday Image, 1996), 195 pages. Fourteenth-century spiritual masterpiece.

David Knight, *His Word: Letting It Take Root and Bear Fruit in Our Lives* (His Way, revised edition, 1994), 81 pages.

*** Robert Knopp, *Gospel Images through Prayer* (Pauline Books and Media). Four volumes, one for each of the gospels.

The Liturgy of the Hours (Moshy Brothers). Four volumes; the complete text of the official edition.

Mariano Magrassi, O.S.B., *Praying the Bible* (Liturgical Press), 144 pages. Draws together the wisdom of medieval and monastic traditions of meditation on Scripture.

John Main, O.S.B., *Word into Silence* (Continuum, 1998), 96 pages. Guide to contemplation by using a prayer-word.

Mary Marrocco, *The Good News Is Love* (St. Mary's Press), 88 pages. Fifteen Scripture passages, with reflections, as a spur to conversation with God.

Anthony Mottola, translator, *The Spiritual Exercises of St. Ignatius* (Doubleday Image, 1964). Influential classic by the founder of the Jesuits.

Basil Pennington, O.C.S.O., *Daily We Touch Him* (Theological Book Service, 1997). Instruction in centering prayer.

Basil Pennington, O.C.S.O., *Lectio Divina: Renewing the Ancient Practice of Praying the Scriptures* (Crossroad, 1998).

David E. Rosage, *Speak, Lord, Your Servant Is Listening: A Daily Guide to Scriptural Prayer* (Servant Books), 131 pages. In this popular prayer guide, Fr. Rosage has arranged short biblical passages, accompanied by brief comments, for each day of the year.

Wilfrid Stinissen, *Nourished by the Word: Reading the Bible Contemplatively* (Liguori). Examines various ways of praying from Scripture.

Page McKean Zyromski, *Pray the Bible* (St. Anthony Messenger Press). Takes the reader step by step through a wide variety of approaches to praying with Scripture.

Appendix One

Additional Bible Study Tools

These references supplement the specific aids listed with chapters 11 (Personal Bible Study), 12 (Group Study), and 13 (Biblical Prayer). The prices are valid for the publication dates. Publishers' phone numbers and websites are listed in Appendix 2.

Bibles With Considerable Study Help for Catholics

The Catholic Study Bible (Oxford University Press, 1990). Contains the NAB text and 600 pages of study materials besides standard NAB notes. Reading guides for every biblical book.

The Catholic Bible: Personal Study Edition (Oxford University Press, 1995). Slightly more introductory in nature than the Catholic Study Bible. Same format, but also includes questions for personal reflection.

The New Jerusalem Bible (Doubleday). Contains short introductory articles to the biblical books, with extensive footnotes and cross-references.

The Catholic Youth Bible (St. Mary's Press, 2000). The NRSV translation with lots of explanatory material, briefly stated, accompanying the biblical text. Not only high school students but many adults would find it helpful.

The Catholic Bible and *The International Student Bible for Catholics* (Sadlier) provide the NAB text with reading guides and explanatory notes.

Other Resources for Reading the Bible

Paul J. Achtemeier and others, editors, *The HarperCollins Bible Dictionary* (Harper San Francisco, 1996), 1250 pages.

The Bible Today. A magazine for the nonprofessional Bible student: contains background, insights, and reflections (Liturgical Press). Six issues annually.

Lawrence Boadt, C.S.P., *Reading the Old Testament* (Paulist Press).

Raymond E. Brown, *Responses to 101 Questions about the Bible* (Paulist, 1990).

Raymond E. Brown, *An Introduction to the New Testament* (Doubleday, 1997), 878 pages.

Raymond E. Brown and others, editors, *The New Jerome Biblical Commentary* (Prentice-Hall, 1989), 1475 pages.

Raymond E. Brown and others, editors, *The New Jerome Bible Handbook* (Liturgical Press, 1992), 416 pages. This is a condensation of the *New Jerome Biblical Commentary*, with many of the notes and academic material removed.

The Collegeville Atlas of the Bible (Liturgical Press, 2000), 144 pages. A guided tour through the Bible from the point of view of historical, geographical, and cultural settings.

The Collegeville Bible Commentary (Liturgical Press, 1983). Pamphlet commentaries on the books of the Old and New Testaments, available singly or in collected forms.

The Collegeville Bible Handbook (Liturgical Press), 352 pages. A condensed version of the *Collegeville Bible Commentary.*

The Collegeville Bible Time-Line (Liturgical Press). Graphic representation of the sequence of events and people in the Bible.

David Noel Freedman and others, editors, *Eerdmans Dictionary of the Bible* (Eerdmans, 2000), 1417 pages.

Lucy Fuchs, *We Were There* (Alba House). Women of the New Testament.

Fulfilled in Your Hearing: The Homily in the Sunday Assembly (USCC, 1982). Statement of the bishops of the United States. Publication No. 850-59, 48 pages.

Daniel J. Harrington, S.J., *Interpreting the Old Testament* and *Interpreting the New Testament* (Liturgical Press). Each book introduces the methods that scholars use in interpreting the Bible.

Wilfrid J. Harrington, O.P., *Key to the Bible* (Alba House). Three volumes which may be purchased individually.

Stephen L. Harris, *Understanding the Bible* (Mayfield, 5th edition, 1999).

Leslie J. Hoppe, *A Guide to the Lands of the Bible* (Liturgical Press, 1999), 400 pages.

Luke Timothy Johnson, *The Writings of the New Testament: An Introduction* (Fortress Press, 1999), revised edition, 694 pages.

Eugene LaVerdiere, S.S.S., *Fundamentalism: A Pastoral Concern* (Liturgical Press, 1983), 8 pages; available at bulk rates.

George Martin, *God's Word: Reading the Gospels* (Our Sunday Visitor Press), 200 pages. Brief, insightful comments on short passages from the Gospels.

J.L. McKenzie, *Dictionary of the Bible* (Macmillan, 1995), 954 pages.

Bruce M. Metzger, *NRSV Exhaustive Concordance* (Nashville: Thomas Nelson Publishers, 1991).

Steve Mueller, *The Seeker's Guide to Reading the Bible* (Loyola Press, 1999).

Giacomo Peregro, S.S.P., *Interdisciplinary Atlas of the Bible* (Alba House), hard cover. Covers the geography, history, sociology, and theology of the Bible. Includes maps.

Pheme Perkins, *Reading the New Testament: An Introduction* (Paulist, revised edition).

John J. Pilch, *The Cultural Dictionary of the Bible* (Liturgical Press, 1999).

John Power, *History of Salvation* (Alba House). An introduction to the Old Testament for beginners.

Margaret Nutting Ralph, *The Bible and the End of the World: Should We Be Afraid?* (Paulist Press). A clear, popularly written interpretation of what the Bible says on this subject, with emphasis on God's love.

Scripture from Scratch (St. Anthony Messenger Press). A program introducing the Bible and scholarly perspectives on it, with videos, workbooks, sourcebooks, and leader's guide.

Patrick J. Sena, C.P.P.S., *Apocalypse: A Guide to the Themes and Teachings of the Book of Revelation* (Alba House).

John Shea, *Stories of Faith* (Thomas More, 1980), 216 pages.

Ronald D. Witherup, *The Bible Companion: A Handbook for Beginners* (Crossroad, 1998).

Appendix Two

How to Contact Catholic Publishers

Alba House
(800) 343-2522
www.albahouse.org

Alba House Communications
(800) 533-2522
www.albahouse.org

Cistercian Publications
Western Michigan University
Kalamazoo, MI 49008
(616) 387-8920

Credence Cassettes
(888) 595-8273

Crossroad Publishing Co.
(800) 395-0690
www.nbnbooks.com

Franciscan Press
websites.quincy.edu/fpress/

God's Word Today
(800) 246-7390

Good Ground Press
(800) 232-5533
www.goodgroundpress.com

Liguori Publications
(800) 325-9521
www.liguori.org

Little Rock Scripture Study
(800) 858-5434
www.littlerockscripture.org

The Liturgical Press
(800) 858-5450
www.litpress.org

Loyola Press
(800) 270-5404
www.loyolapress.com

New City Press
(800) 462-5980
www.newcitypress.com

Our Sunday Visitor Press
(800) 348-2440
www.osv.com

Paulist Press
(800) 218-1903
www.paulistpress.com

William H. Sadlier, Inc.
(800) 221-5175
www.sadlier.com

St. Anthony Messenger Press
(800) 488-0488
www.americancatholic.org

St. Bede's Publications
(800) 507-1000
www.cbpa.org/publisher/bedes.htm

St. Mary's Press
(800) 344-9225
www.smp.org

Servant Publications
(800) 486-8505

Share the Word
(800) 237-5515
www.sharetheword.net

Thomas More Press
180 N. Wabash
Chicago, IL 60601

United States Catholic Conference
Publications Office
(800) 235-8722
www.nccbuscc.org

The Word Among Us
(800) 775-9673
www.wau.org

Glossary*

Additional Bible Study Tools

Allegory—Extended comparison (for example, Mt 21:33-46). See *Parable*.

Apocalyptic—Form of writing popular 200 B.C. to A.D. 200, characterized by visions, symbols, and the revelation of mysteries about the final divine victory; from Greek *apocalypsis*, "revelation."

Apocrypha—Old Testament books considered inspired Scripture by Catholics but not by Protestants and Jews: from Greek *apocryphon* "hidden." See *Deuterocanonical books*.

Armageddon—Symbolic location of the final decisive victory over evil according to Rv 16:16; from Hebrew *har megiddo*, "mountain of Megiddo."

Asia Minor—Literally "little Asia," the western peninsula of Asia, today comprised mainly of Turkey, the scene of much of St. Paul's missionary activity and letter writing.

Some of these terms are explained more thoroughly elsewhere in the book (See Index).

Assyria—Mesopotamian empire which conquered the northern kingdom of Israel in 721 B.C., taking inhabitants into exile; fell to Babylon in 605 B.C.

Baal—Canaanite god.

Babylon—Mesopotamian empire which conquered the southern kingdom of Judah in 587 B.C., taking inhabitants into exile; fell to Persia in 539 B.C. See *Exile*.

Canon—List of writings defined as inspired Scripture; the Greek for "measure, norm."

Captivity epistles—Letters of Paul written from prison: Philippians, Philemon, Colossians, Ephesians.

Catholic epistles—New Testament writings without specific addresses and therefore considered directed to the universal ("catholic") Church: James, 1 and 2 Peter, 1, 2, and 3 John, Jude.

Codex—Ancient manuscript in which separate pages are bound together as in a modern book, rather than in a scroll; a Latin word for "book."

Concordance—Book listing words used in the Bible in alphabetical order with verse references; a tool for locating quotations.

Covenant—Agreement, pact.

Dead Sea Scrolls—Ancient manuscripts of Old Testament and nonbiblical writings discovered at Qumran near the Dead Sea. See *Essenes* and *Qumran*.

Decalogue—The Ten Commandments; from the Greek for "Ten Words."

Deuterocanonical books—Seven Old Testament books (Sirach, Wisdom, 1 and 2 Maccabees, Judith, Tobit, Baruch) and parts of two others (Daniel, Esther) considered inspired Scripture by Catholics but not by Protestants and Jews; from the Greek for "second canonical (group)." See *Apocrypha*.

Deuteronomist history—Books written from the theological perspective typical of the Book of Deuteronomy: Joshua, Judges, 1 and 2 Samuel, 1 and 2 Kings.

Diaspora—The disperson of Jews outside the land of Israel; also areas outside Israel where Jews settled or were exiled; from the Greek for "dispersion."

Elders—Influential members of the Jewish community who were involved in decision-making. See *Presbyter*.

Eschatology—Having to do with the "end time," the messianic age, and in Christian thought, eternal life in heaven; from Greek *eschaton* "end."

Essenes—A strict sect of Jews which separated from the mainstream. See *Qumran*.

Exegesis—The practice of biblical interpretation; the implementation of *hermeneutics*.

Exile—The deportation of the Jews to Babylon (587-538 B.C.) after the destruction of Jerusalem and Solomon's Temple.

Form criticism—Method of biblical interpretation involving analysis of the original oral forms of materials incorporated into the Gospels.

Gloss—A brief correction or remark inserted by a scribe in the margin or between the lines of a manuscript.

Gnosticism—Doctrinal system claiming a secret knowledge of God and the mystery of salvation; from Greek *gnosis*, "knowledge."

Haggada—Rabbinic method of biblical commentary directed to ethical or devotional purposes.

Halakah—Rabbinic method of biblical commentary directed to legal questions.

Hellenism—The influence of Greek culture and language promoted by the conquests of Alexander the Great; from Greek *Hellas*, "Greece."

Hermeneutics—Principles and methods of biblical interpretation. See *Exegesis*.

Holocaust—Temple offering in which an animal or bird is slaughtered and burned (Lv 1).

Israel—Northern kingdom comprising the ten tribes which seceded following Solomon's death (1 Kgs 12); to distinguish from Judah, the southern kingdom; name used also to denote the whole land or people. See *Judah*.

Jehovah—Mistaken pronunciation of God's name, Yahweh, formulated by combining the Hebrew consonants *yhwh* (*jhvh*) with the vowels of *Adonai,* "Lord." See *Tetragrammaton; Yahweh*.

Josephus—Flavius Josephus, Jewish historian (A.D. 37-100).

Judah—Tribe of David which became the core of the southern kingdom after the split following Solomon's death. See *Israel*.

Judge—Local leader in the era between Joshua and Saul (1200-1050 B.C.).

Koine—Form of Greek common to the Mediterranean area after 300 B.C., as distinct from classical Greek; the language of the New Testament; from the Greek for "common."

Koran—Holy book of Islam.

Levites—Members of the tribe of Levi assigned to secondary duties in the Temple.

Logion—Technical word for individual utterances of Jesus· the Greek for "saying" (pl. *logia*).

LXX—Symbol for *Septuagint* (from Latin *septuaginta,* "seventy"), title given to the ancient Greek translation of the Old Testament; from the legendary seventy-two translators.

Massoretes—Medieval Jewish scholars who developed the Massoretic Text (MT); from Hebrew *massoret,* "tradition."

Messiah—Hebrew for "Anointed One," a title of Israelite kings; the expected savior; in Greek, "Christos" (Christ).

Midrash—Rabbinical method of interpreting a biblical text to make it applicable to a latter generation; from Hebrew *darash,* "to seek."

Millennium—Thousand years; from Latin *mille,* "thousand."

MT—Massoretic Text: standard text of the Hebrew scriptures produced by medieval Jewish scholars. See *Massoretes.*

Palimpsest—Parchment imperfectly erased and used again in such a way that the older text is still decipherable; from the Greek for "scraped again."

Parable—Story or example usually emphasizing one point or comparison, drawing the listener into a new vision of life. See *Allegory.*

Parousia—Traditional term for Christ's coming in glory; the Greek for "appearance" or "arrival."

Pastoral epistles—Paul's letters to Timothy and Titus.

Pentateuch—First five books of the Bible; from the Greek for "five books"; the Hebrew *Torah.*

Pharisees—Lay reform group within Judaism; from Hebrew *perushim,* "separate ones."

Phylacteries—Tiny scrolls containing biblical texts, worn on the forehead and the left arm in fulfillment of Exodus 13:16 and Deuteronomy 6:8; from the Greek for "guard."

Presbyter—Same as *elder,* from the Greek for "older person."

Qumran—Site near the Dead Sea where an Essene monastery and ancient scrolls were found. See *Dead Sea Scrolls; Essenes.*

Rapture—Erroneous doctrine that faithful Christians will be "raptured" (snatched) out of the world and later return for a thousand-year reign.

Redaction criticism—Method of biblical interpretation used especially in the Gospels to discover an evangelist's purpose through his redaction (editing) of his sources.

Sadducees—Jewish religious group composed of members of the priestly ruling class and their supporters.

Samaria—Royal city of the northern kingdom of Israel which gave its name to the whole area; by the time of Jesus a more limited region between Galilee and Judea, from which it was separated by religious differences.

Samaritans—Inhabitants of Samaria sharing the biblical tradition but considered heretical and hostile by postexilic Jews.

Sanhedrin—Jewish decision-making body composed of the high priest and seventy other leaders; patterned on the council of Moses and his seventy elders.

Seder—Festive ritual meal of the first night of Passover; from the Hebrew for "order."

Septuagint—Ancient Greek translation of the Old Testament. See *LXX*.

Shema—First word and title of the traditional daily prayer of the Jews: "Hear, O Israel ..." (Dt 6:4-5).

Sheol—In ancient Hebrew thought, the place of the spirits of the dead: the "underworld."

Sitz-im-Leben—German phrase meaning "situation in life" used as a technical term in discussing the context (of Jesus, the later Christian community, or the evangelist) in which a Gospel passage was produced.

Tabernacle—Tent, especially the wilderness sanctuary (Ex 40:1-11).

Targum—Expanded translation of the Hebrew Scriptures into Aramaic; the Hebrew for "translation."

Tell—Archeological term for a hill or mound created by long occupation of a site; Hebrew for "mound."

Tetragrammaton—The Hebrew name of God, *Yhwh*; from the Greek for "four letters." See *Jehovah*; *Yahweh*.

Textus receptus—Biblical text considered normative for translation; especially the Greek New Testament text accepted as standard from the sixteenth to the nineteenth centuries; the Latin for "received text."

Torah—The Law: usually equated with the first five books of the Bible; the Hebrew for "law." See *Pentateuch*.

Transjordan—Literally "across the Jordan," an older name for the present-day country of Jordan.

Version—Translation.

Vulgate—St. Jerome's translation of the Bible from the original languages into Latin; from *vulgata editio*: "widely circulated edition."

Wadi—Stream that is dry part of the year.

Yahweh—Ancient Hebrew name for God. See *Jehovah*; *Tetragrammaton*.

Zealots—Jewish revolutionaries bent on the expulsion of Rome from Israel.

Zion—Ancient name for Jerusalem.

Index